Jane

Big, good laugh!

J. Eng

Innovation at the Speed of Laughter

INNOVATION

AT THE SPEED OF LAUGHTER

8 Secrets to World Class Idea Generation

JOHN SWEENEY

AND THE BRAVE NEW WORKSHOP

Aerialist
Press

ISBN 0-9762184-0-2

Library of Congress Catalog Number: 2004107469

Published in the United States of America
Printed in Canada

First Printing: June 2004

08   07   06   05   04   5   4   3   2   1

Dustjacket design by Kyle G. Hunter
Book design by Wendy Holdman
Composition by Stanton Publication Services, Inc.

Aerialist Press, or Publishing Without a Net
Minneapolis, MN
www.aerialistpress.com

The book is dedicated to Dudley Riggs

and anyone who has ever worked at the

Brave New Workshop

and that lovable innovative character,

Robert (Bobby) Brady.

"My dear friends, you are now about to enter

the nerve center of the entire Wonka Factory.

Inside this room, all of my dreams become realities.

And some of my realities become dreams.

And almost everything you will see is eatible. Edible.

I mean you can eat almost everything."

WILLY WONKA

Contents

Preface

In early 1991 I began taking classes in the art of improvisational theatre, mostly as a stress reliever I guess. I was probably working a little too hard and needed something to distract me from the daily grind of corporate real estate. Life wasn't bad though. I had a great house, a high paying job, and an exceptional social life. I thought that taking a class in improvisation might also be a way to fulfill my need to be "the funny guy."

I remember everything about that first class—every exercise we did and, most importantly, every emotion I felt as I became more excited, more curious, and more intrigued with this quirky little art form. In the next two years, I became consumed with improvisation. I couldn't get enough. It seemed more than just a vehicle to perform; it stirred me, it was undeniable.

In October of 1993, it seemed as though I was fully addicted to improvisation as I made the decision to leave the 40th floor of the IDS Tower in Minneapolis, Minnesota, and my job as a commercial real estate consultant, to become a full-time resident member of the Dudley Riggs Brave New Workshop Comedy Theatre. My starting salary was $200 per week before taxes. I sold my home, turned in my company car, and started driving a 1989 Bonneville that my brother gave me. I had no idea where this improvisational path would lead but I knew that if I didn't follow it, it would be something I'd regret for the rest of my life. So there I was—twenty-eight, single, and a full-time comedic actor. Where would this lead me?

Eleven years later, my wife, Jenni Lilledahl, and I own that very same theatre. We have a wonderful marriage, a beautiful new son, and a life we wouldn't change for anything. If I had to attribute this phenomenal journey to one thing, it would be improvisation. Since that first class, I have slowly incorporated the values and principles of improvisation into my stage work, my relationships, and how I run my business.

In March of 1997 when we purchased the Brave New Workshop Theatre from its founder, Dudley Riggs, it had gross revenues of a little over $200,000 per year. Seven years later, we will exceed $2 million per year. We have grown this wonderful company from five employees to having more than fifty people on our weekly payroll list. The educational arm of the company, the Brave New Institute, has grown from twelve students to more than 275. Our corporate services division has gone from being almost non-existent to having a reputation as a national leader in corporate entertainment, training, and keynote speaking.

I wish I could say that this level of growth and success is a clear representation of my competence, vision, and managerial skills. The truth is, in all three areas, I am average at best. Improvisation is the reason we have achieved such success. If I have done anything to play a role in the last ten years of my life it would be that I have been able to bridge my understanding of improvisational theatre into both the personal and business sides of my life. By simply following the secrets you are about to read, I have been able to surround myself with incredibly competent and loyal employees and produce products that generally surpass our customers' and clients' expectations.

My hope is that you will be able to use these same secrets to improve your innovation and the quality of your work and your life. Hang on and enjoy the ride.

Acknowledgments

In the spirit of the ensemble creation process, this book was written by a team. Everyone at the Brave New Workshop contributed to make this book a reality. The team that assisted most in the process was Dawn Hopkins, Jen Bellmont, and Troy Alexander. Their immense talent and gentle tolerance allowed me to once again create something that is beyond my own capabilities.

I am grateful to them.

Introduction

Since 1958, the Brave New Workshop Theatre has created smart, edgy, and innovative comedy on a yearly, monthly, weekly, daily, and sometimes hourly basis. If you were to stand in the lobby of our small, storefront theatre after one of our shows, you'd hear the following comments: "How did they think of that?" "This show was better than the last show!" "How do they come up with that stuff?" "That was the funniest thing I have ever seen!" We've been consistently hearing these comments from more than three million customers for over forty-five years.

Brave New Workshop (BNW) staff, instructors, and performers have developed the secrets of its unique brand of improvisation—and the principles and philosophies that go with it—for generations. From students in our classrooms to actors and writers on our stage to the audiences in our seats, the BNW and all who have worked there have been able to create and recreate a viable product without compromising our standards of intelligent, issue-based comedy.

Now I'd like to share those secrets with you.

I wrote this book to ensure the wisdom, traditions, and processes that have been established by the Brave New Workshop Theatre will be recorded and preserved. As an improviser, I believe the next scene is a direct result of all the scenes that came before it. I feel it is time to give the idea generation process its due respect. I want to ensure that our innovative process continues to grow and evolve.

The Brave New Workshop adheres to the secrets you're about to be introduced to as much for profitability as for creative expression. Like any business, the theatre needs to ensure continued existence by creating experiences and products that ensure customer excitement and loyalty. Relying on the principles included in this book, the theatre operates as one of only a few self-sustaining, non-profit theatre organizations and does not rely on corporate or government funding.

While everyone who works at the Brave New Workshop is passionate about developing innovative comedy, I remind myself daily that I need to approach the BNW product and business process like any other company in any other industry. I am constantly mindful of the:

1. marketability of the end product,

2. expense-to-income ratio of the product development,

3. evaluation of which projects produce the most bang for the buck, and

4. reinforcement of the brand.

I am also writing this book because I have been asked to share the theatre's secrets of innovation. The idea generation process and secrets I am revealing are applicable to any individual, group, or organization that needs to create the next great idea. I believe the path to each person's most creative self is unique for every individual, and therefore every organization. I hope this book gives you more perspective, and perhaps more insight, to your own innovative path. Perhaps something within these pages will create an "aha" moment—a breakthrough that leads to greater confidence and comfort with your own creative self. On a daily basis, BNW adult improvisation students and BNW employees have these "aha" moments—they stumble upon, or discover, or accidentally come up with wonderful, creative, and incredible ideas. As students and staff are exposed to these secrets, they can clearly identify an increase in their innovative productivity. I sincerely hope this book helps you with that same transformation.

I also hope this book will draw attention to the Brave New Workshop Theatre and honor its founder Dudley Riggs. For nearly five decades this magical comedy theatre remained relatively unknown because Dudley adapted a truly Minnesotan style of life. He did not need to let the world know about his little theatre, let alone brag about the wonderful work the staff and casts created or the famous alumni they trained. Ridiculously successful individuals like Al Franken (author/performer/activist), Mo Collins (writer/performer—*Mad TV)*, Tom Sherhoman (writer—*Mr. Magoo, Change of Seasons*), Peter Tolan (writer—*Analyze This*; writer/producer—*The Larry Sanders Show, Murphy Brown, Analyze This*), Pat Proft (writer—*Scary Movie, Naked Gun*), Irv Letofsky (theatre critic—*Los Angeles Times*), Linda Wallem (writer/producer—*That '70s Show*), Peter MacNicol (actor—*Sophie's Choice, Ally McBeal*), Mike McManus (writer—*M.A.S.H.*), Nancy Steen (head writer—*Happy Days*), Melissa Peterman (co-star—*Reba*), Cedric Yarbrough (actor—*Reno 911!*) and countless others have all learned the following secrets and honed their skills on BNW stages.

I do not intend for this book to teach people how to create comedy or perform improvisational theatre. The BNW and I use comedy and improvisation as *our* way to illustrate *our* secrets because it is what we do, and continues to be our core business. It is what we know best. For some of us it is all we know.

Creating improvisation and sketch comedy for our stages is just a small portion of what the Brave New Workshop has accomplished. The BNW has taken the innovation process outside the theatre and developed products for other companies. This "corporate" line of services has been a wonderful by-product of a rich comedic tradition and is currently the fastest-growing part of the BNW business. Because so many people have asked BNW staff and cast to share what they know, we have found ourselves in vastly varied and wonderfully uncommon situations in which we can contribute. For instance:

1. We helped General Mills' Yoplait division find their next great product idea.

2. We worked with the employees of 3M Corporation to help them define what innovative leadership means to them.

3. We helped Hewlett Packard find levity and celebration in the challenges of the company's merger with Compaq.

4. We helped the Disney Company develop programming activities for young guests aboard their cruise ships.

5. We helped Sprint PCS excite their sales force about the most innovative technology in the company's history.

6. We helped Texas Instruments change the way they look at employee diversity.

7. We helped the Minnesota Timberwolves organization approach their customers differently and taught their mascot, Crunch, how to be more creative and spontaneous when interacting with Wolves' fans.

8. We helped the engineering division of Pillsbury embrace the post-merger culture of General Mills.

9. We helped Glaxo Pharmaceuticals explain the benefits of their post-chemotherapy drug, Zofran.

10. We helped the employees of the Rainforest Café learn how to engage in conversational selling.

11. We helped the executives of GMAC-ERS explain the benefits of Risk Management.

12. We helped Better Homes and Gardens Real Estate celebrate twenty-five years of success.

13. We helped warm up the audience for Zig Ziglar, Kenny Loggins, Queen Latifah, and Tom Jones.

14. We helped the coordinators of the Lutheran World Mission work better together and, in turn, educate and feed more of the world's needy.

15. We shared the principles of improvisation with the most innovative people in the world of medical products at Medtronic to help them develop new ways to keep us all alive!

The secrets contained in this book are the basis of how we add value to all of these situations.

Like an ongoing improvisational scene, the Brave New Workshop truly is the product of continuous innovation and hard work. Because we are able to consistently reinvent our products, and ourselves, the BNW brand has become synonymous with quality satirical theatre. Our success is clearly the result of *all* of the people who have worked here and contributed to the "scene." Thousands of people have given small and large chunks of their lives to help this theatre adhere to its motto of "Promiscuous Hostility, Positive Neutrality." Some of them gave hours, others gave years, some gave decades, and a couple of them were actually paid.

A note about the format of this book.

Each chapter begins with a script sample from a Brave New Workshop sketch comedy show. We decided to begin each chapter with a script because: (1) it offers a real example of a product we produce using the 8 Secrets and the funnel process and (2) it will allow you to begin each chapter with laughter. Although sometimes hard to define, we absolutely believe that the infusion of laughter can increase learning, creativity, innovation, and productivity.

There is no magic pill, a single event, or even a book that will instantly give you more creativity and innovation. But if you embrace these secrets and utilize our process, you and the people you work with will increase the potential and probability of finding the next great profitable idea. And who knows? One of you might be the originator of the next "ridiculous," "crazy," or "foolish" idea—ideas like penicillin, space travel, or the personal computer.

▲

**"We are the music makers,
we are the dreamers of dreams."**

Willy Wonka

The

SECRETS

of BNW Creativity

SECRET 1

Accepting All Ideas

BRAVE NEW WORKSHOP THEATRE

DATE: 01.19.02

SHOW: We Moved Our Cheese, or Hindsight is 2605 Hennepin

TITLE: "Cubicle Etiquette"

DRAFT: FINAL

PREMISE:
Cubicle culture has taken on such a life, it now needs social rules

SETTING:
A generic office set of a low-budget, in-house industrial training film

CHARACTERS:
CHIP and HONEY: Cheesy industrial actors with no personalities but great teeth

CORKY: A stiff actor portraying the personification of an inanimate object

VARIOUS OFFICE PLAYERS: Actors not pretty enough to be successful in industrials, but are often called in to play "real people"

(Video clip—swishing noise accompanies swirling graphics and voice over saying, "Cubicle Etiquette and You. It's totally cubular, man." Bad music begins to play. Lights up on stage where video is occurring live. CHIP and HONEY enter. They are in the middle of a fake conversation. They "happen" to see the audience.)

CHIP

Oh, hi there. So glad you could join us today. I'm Chip.

HONEY

And I'm Honey. Welcome to Cubicle Etiquette and You.

CHIP

It's totally cubular, man.

HONEY

In today's business world, the "open-office plan"
is becoming more and more popular.

CHIP

That means cubicles to you and me.

HONEY

Exactly, Chip, and in that world there are definite
cubicle "do's" and cubicle "dont's."

CHIP

For instance, Honey and I are friends, so I feel
confident standing this close to her.

HONEY

Exactly, Chip. But if I didn't know you well, I might feel
that my space has been invaded, which leads us to our
first set of guidelines concerning cubicle privacy.

Rule number one: Don't be a "space invader."

CHIP

It's a fun video game, but it can lead to office
dysfunction or even litigation.

HONEY

Let's check out "The Office," and see if we
can find more "do's" and "dont's."

(They cross to opposite sides of stage, as Corky the Cubicle enters.)

HONEY

This is Corky the Cubicle. Corky's going to help us
learn our rules of cubicle etiquette.

CHIP

Rule number two—

CORKY

Don't "prairie dog."

CHIP

Popping your head over the cubicle wall is
a very invasive gesture . . .

(Person in center cubicle is doing a ridiculous interpretation of Prairie Dogging, jumping up and down, popping his or her head over the cubicle wall.)

CHIP

. . . and can lead to angry neighbors.

(Woman in cubicle throws grenade over wall, sound of explosion.)

CHIP

But if he can't just pop his head over the wall, how will
he communicate with his co-workers?

HONEY

Well, that's rule number three.

CORKY

Always ask permission to enter a cubicle.

(Person who has been jumping, walks over to cubicle, still rubbing head, mimes asking to be invited into cubicle. Cubicle dweller nods yes, and person enters, but they stand very close to cubicle dweller, sniffing hair, etc.)

CHIP

Whoa, Tiger! Once in the cubicle, be aware of blocking
the entrance in a threatening manner.

(Upon hearing Chip's warning, guest steps away from the dweller and the entrance. Dweller and guest look at Chip and give the thumbs up sign.)

HONEY

Now that we know to ask permission to enter a cubicle,
let's talk about when to do it.

CHIP

Rule number four.

CORKY

Never interrupt someone who is deep in thought.

(Woman from first cubicle has entered other cubicle without asking. Man who is deep in thought maces her in the face.)

HONEY AND CHIP

Uh-oh!

CHIP

She's in trouble now.

HONEY

Remember, a blind office worker is an inefficient office worker.

(CHIP and HONEY laugh as guest staggers around the stage in agony.)

CHIP

When you have thirty or forty people packed in a fifteen square
foot room, it's important to be mindful of noise.

HONEY

Because no matter how hard you pretend,
fake walls can't keep out sound.

CHIP

Exactly, Honey, and that brings us to rule number five.

CORKY

Avoid annoying noises.

(MAN enters with a saw and begins playing it.)

WOMAN

Get out of my head!

CHIP

Finally, let's talk about decor, and rule number six . . .

CORKY

Decorate your cubicle in a non-offensive manner.

(WOMAN enters with a great big poster of Hitler.)

HONEY

Look around. Are you putting up things that
might be deemed offensive by a co-worker?

(Person looks at items, realizes they might be offensive, sneaks offstage.)

CHIP

I think she's got it.

(As CHIP and HONEY cross center stage, they laugh, then stop abruptly. As they speak, others exit.)

CHIP

But cubicle etiquette is no laughing matter. Cubicle culture
is the wave of the present and the future.

HONEY

So get used to it. The old dream of your own space
with walls and a window is gone.

CHIP

And the future is here. The then is now. So hang on
and go for the ride of your life.

HONEY

And remember, "Cubicle Etiquette and You."

CHIP

It's totally cubular, man.

(They laugh as lights black out.)

Explanation of the Secret

Most often when people hear me talk about accepting all ideas they assume that I mean to accept ideas that they understand, are comfortable with, or that seem to make sense. In actuality, I really do mean *all* ideas—perhaps most importantly, the very ideas that you don't understand and aren't familiar with and that make you uncomfortable or that seem ridiculous or illogical. Remember, if the idea seems odd to you, most likely it seems normal to someone else and vice versa.

Improvisers accept that whatever idea presents itself is a gift. Not having an idea or "gift" at the beginning of an improvisational scene leaves you alone, onstage, in front of hundreds of people who have paid $22 to come see you be funny. Not being able to find the next funny thing to say or do is one of the most humbling and horrible experiences a person can have. I personally begin to hear the individual heartbeats of each audience member. I often hear my father's voice reminding me that I should have stayed in real estate. At this point, if a fellow improviser enters the scene with an idea—any idea—it feels as if I have been thrown a life preserver, or in improv terminology, I've been given a gift. As you can imagine, in this situation I am never overcome with the need to judge that idea. I am grateful for it and accept it immediately. The challenge is to be able to treat ideas with the same level of gratefulness and acceptance when we are not in a situation of need.

Within the BNW idea generation process, I have found that accepting ideas not only demonstrates respect for the idea, it also demonstrates respect for the person who generated it. Conversely, when someone negates an idea, they almost always indirectly negate the individual who presented the idea.

In terms of productivity, a consistent and clear acceptance of people's ideas creates the expectation that their ideas will be met with a positive reaction, rather than disagreement or judgment. As a result, people tend to increase the number of ideas they produce, and consequently, the quality of the end product. As proven time and time again from Pavlov's dogs to child development, positive reinforcement elicits a faster rate of learning and a quicker response to consistent stimuli.

I found that when the status quo of the environment is to accept all ideas, people become accustomed to the positive reinforcement, and respond by producing more and better ideas in order to re-create the positive experience. If a person is used to, or worse yet, expects, their idea will most likely be rejected, they have a tendency to create fewer ideas in order to minimize the occurrences of negative experiences. There is a huge difference between ac-cepting someone's idea and executing it. Most individuals are much more interested in having their ideas heard and respected than having them implemented. Accepting an idea simply lets a person know you heard them and will treat their idea as a valid possibility.

> *There is a huge difference between accepting someone's idea and executing it.*

A typical improv scene lasts between two and three minutes. Within that timeframe, improvisers must work together as a team in order to figure out and declare who they are, where they are, and what they want to accomplish. They must define and distribute individual roles, create some comedic conflict, and resolve the scene. They must do all of this based on a random suggestion from the audience, who expects the improvised scene to be hilarious. Due to the inherent speed and pressure of this process, improvisers have learned (over many years) that if a team member chooses not to accept an idea, huge amounts of precious time are wasted, and the scene stops moving forward toward a successful solution.

I have to admit that at times I become cynical and almost want to believe it is human nature *not* to accept the ideas of others. I find that the skill of accepting all ideas is perhaps one of the hardest to teach to both improvisers and business professionals. I am reminded of our tendency to disagree when I witness improvisers passionately arguing about whose made-up idea was right or wrong. Although nothing that an improviser does exists within "the real world," we still find the need to defend our imagination and disagree with others. Some of these arguments in which the subject matter is make-believe are as humorous as the scenes we perform.

I remember a post-show discussion in which we were critiquing each other's work and evaluating our improv performance. In the course of the show, an actor had come forward miming as if they were holding a large fish. Another actor in the scene reacted to the first actor's declaration with a reference to the movie *Jaws*. The actor holding the fish literally stopped the scene and glared at the actor who made the *Jaws* comment. Instantly, the stage was filled with an awkward sense of confusion. Another actor had to stop the scene and start a new one. During the post-show discussion, the actor who made the *Jaws* comment asked why the first actor had reacted so strongly to her response. The actor who had mimed holding the fish was still angry and pointed out that earlier in the scene she had clearly "set the scene" in a freshwater environment. It was "wrong" for the second actor to inaccurately decide that the fish she was holding was a shark. How typical of human nature to contradict others' ideas, even when the basis of the contradiction is about a subject matter completely make-believe.

Most of the memorable, best-improvised scenes I have been a part of started with ideas I did not understand, was not comfortable with, or considered atypical or illogical. Yet, these scenes stand out in my mind as being incredibly successful, undeniably funny, and vivid examples of what can happen when we accept all ideas.

Identifying the Corporate Need

Oftentimes when I am working with a company that needs help accepting new ideas, the company has a wide range of employee ages and levels of experience. A common scenario is when seasoned employees who have been working in the same capacity for many years negate ideas from less experienced co-workers. Perhaps they feel "they have already tried that idea" or "management will never go for it." The reverse is also often true in that newer employees might negate the ideas of a veteran employee because they assume the older employee is jaded or set in their ways. Both of these preconceived notions can prohibit new ideas from bearing fruit. New or inexperienced employees may lose interest in idea generation. Additionally, the amount of experience and wisdom that can transfer from veteran employees to newbies is drastically reduced. Employee to employee learning is stifled before it ever gets a foothold in creating a cohesive team.

Again, let's remind ourselves that there is a huge difference between accepting someone's idea and implementing it. We are not talking about approving a budget or assigning a staff or creating a policy; those types of implementable characteristics are a long way off.

Success Story: Hewlett Packard

Hewlett-Packard (HP) is a company known for its innovation in developing computer printers. Each year they have the task of educating their sales force in the many features of the new printers they are bringing to market. HP asked the Brave New Workshop to help them deliver the information regarding their new models to their sales force. Traditionally, HP approached the printer training in a classic academic format with expert instructors delivering classroom style PowerPoint presentations to the audience. We presented dozens of nontraditional and distinctive concepts that could be used to relay the same information to the audience in a more innovative way. Hewlett-Packard was able to accept these drastically different ideas and ultimately implemented a training format utilizing our actors and their instructors in a "David Letterman meets Oprah" talk show style. The audience heard from expert instructors in character as guests on a fictitious television show. HP and the BNW did not compromise the quality or quantity of the technical information the sales force needed. The information was intermingled with message-driven comedy and delivered in a memorable way. In addition to receiving the information about the printers, the sales force was motivated by the innovative approach. If the leaders of Hewlett-Packard were not actively practicing the secret of accepting all ideas, they would have missed this powerful opportunity.

▲

"The audience loved the show! Your ability to masterfully blend comedy with education was the perfect answer."

Noel Samlaska, Coordinator,
Annual Sales Training Conference, Hewlett Packard

The Secret of Accepting All Ideas is Working When

- You notice a drastic increase in the number of possible ideas you have to choose from when you enter the next stage of the idea generation process.
- You and your employees gain insight into how far you can stretch your own "comfort zones" and how open-minded you can become.
- You experience the "Jiffy Pop" syndrome in which ideas are produced faster than you can even record them.
- You start to notice that perhaps you had a past tendency to disagree with ideas for no apparent reason and work to change that.
- You hear your employees make comments about how it seems they are receiving more respect.
- You are surprised by the idea output from even your most shy or introverted team members.
- You recognize the foundation has been set for a status-less environment.

The secret of Accepting All Ideas is most effective in training sessions that deal with the subjects of innovation and leadership.

BNW Product Application

Like any company, we can get into a rut of simply doing things a certain way because that is how it was always done in the past. The following is an example of how accepting ideas that seemed odd at first can help you organically discover new ideas and new practices that are better than your old ones. In our example, the new ideas are refreshing to our loyal customers—many who have seen several of our productions and appreciate it anytime we re-invent ourselves.

We were in the final rehearsal stages of a show on our Minneapolis stage entitled *Prozac, It's What's for Dinner, or Let the Side Effects Begin*. We had most of the show written and were working on developing the opening number. Traditionally, we began our shows with a musical number full of energy and excitement. This "classic" Brave New Workshop opening often incorporated the actual title of the show and personified the theme to be carried on throughout the entire show. As we were brainstorming possible ideas of what could happen at the beginning of the show, one of the actors asked, "What if nothing happened?" At first we all laughed, and then realized the actor was not making a joke. Someone said, "If nothing happened, the audience would feel uncomfortable and not know what to do!" "Yeah," another actor said, "They'd go crazy," and still another actor added, "They would be the ones who needed Prozac!" And we were on to something! We eventually decided to start the show with lights up on a bare stage. Two actors were planted in the front row and, after a lengthy, uncomfortable pause, they began to comment on the fact that nothing was happening on stage. To this day, our audience members consider it one of our best openings.

BNW Management Application

In this section of each chapter, I cite real examples of how the secret is being used as a management tool within our company.

By accepting all ideas in the initial stage of brainstorming you can create nontraditional scenarios—some of which can lead to an innovative solution. For example, one dilemma many theatres face is deciding whether they should form their business as a nonprofit organization or a for-profit corporation. There are benefits, both financial and creative, to both of these classifications. As the staff and I rolled this question through our idea development process, we found ourselves asking, "Why can't we be both?" After consulting with our law firm, other theatres, and the Internal Revenue Service, we realized that not only could we do both, it was a great idea! We formed a Subchapter S. Corporation and a 501c3 nonprofit. We also created an IRS-approved management agreement between the two companies, which enables them to legally work together. It is one of the reasons the BNW is still a self-sustaining theatre and self-funding company. It also ensures our educational and outreach programs continue.

From Our Employees

Within each chapter of the book, I include excerpts taken directly from testimonials submitted by our employees.

> One of the things we are most proud of in our workplace is we have created an environment in which we accept all ideas. This mentality of equality in ideas and personnel clearly starts at the top of our organization and influences everyone on staff. The executives and managers of our company are well practiced and extremely consistent in accepting the ideas of the people they manage. This system of top-down acceptance is different than in any of my previous workplaces. It is a conscious management choice

and a behavior that we all try to maintain and improve. Like many other aspects of our workplace, our automatic acceptance of ideas comes directly from practicing the art of improvisation.

After interviewing and training hundreds of businesses, my husband John Sweeney realized that perhaps there was a fundamental flaw in the traditional process of corporate idea sharing from an employee to his or her supervisor or manager. It seemed as though there were characteristics of the process that reduced the employees' abilities to freely share ideas with anyone above them in the organizational chart.

Countless individuals expressed the pressure and fear they experienced when they were asked to share an idea with someone who had more experience, made more money, had a more important title, or a larger office.

In constructing the Brave New Workshop workplace culture, we decided to specifically reverse the scenario. It dawned on us, the pressure should not be on the less experienced person or the person who makes less money or has less of a title—the pressure should be on the supervisor or manager or boss. So that's how it works here. The challenge, or pressure, is mostly on the upper level management to build skills in accepting all ideas. We pride ourselves in being improvisational leaders that respond to all of the ideas of the employees we manage, positively, and in a way that increases their potential to produce more and better ideas. The one thing we consistently hear from our employees is they work in an environment in which their ideas are accepted and respected.

Jenni Lilledahl, Owner of the Brave New Workshop
Executive Director, Brave New Institute

SECRET 2

Deferring Judgment

To hear the following song performed, visit speedoflaughter.com and click on the audio file. Or, buy our CD, "Songs of the Brave New Workshop, Best of Vol. 1."

BRAVE NEW WORKSHOP THEATRE

DATE: 01.18.01

SHOW: How to Try in Business Without Really Succeeding, or A Cubicle Named Desire

TITLE: "Ballad"

DRAFT: FINAL

PREMISE:
There is no greater hero than the guy who can fix your copier—so let's immortalize him in song!

SETTING:
A combination Irish pub/dimensional gate that allows travel through time and space.

CHARACTERS:
BALLADEER: An Irish revolutionary who is short on good material. He occasionally has flashbacks to his days when he sang about a more noble cause.

SEAMUS: A fine Irish fella with an uncanny ability to repair copiers.

TRAGOS: A group of Irish peasants who act out the various characters in the story of Seamus.

(Lights up on BALLADEER. He sings the story of SEAMUS. As he does, the TRAGOS reenact the events. The music begins with a recognizable Irish reel that segues and builds into a traditional Irish drumbeat with full orchestration.)

BALLADEER
Gather about your wee ones,
and wake the sleeping old,

'Tis a stormy night and the time is right
for a tale that must be told,

I sing now of a hero,
a man of steely heart,

But he had to go to trade school
'cause he never was that smart.

With tools in hand he'd greet you
with a furrowed brow and frown,

Cause he's the guy you have to call
when your copier breaks down.

His prices were always high
but he always was a fair man,

His name was Seamus O'Leary,
certified Xerox repairman.

Sing lie, li lie, li lie, li lie lie lie lie, lie li lie li lie . . .
lie li lie, li lie li lie lie lie lie lie lie lie

As a young boy he was quick and strong,
but he always was a loner.

Some say the banshees replaced his blood
with eighteen pints of toner.

So off he went to America
with little more than his name.

He graduated from DeVry
and went out seeking fame.

The work came hard and fast,
young Seamus was in luck,

Cause anyone who's used one knows
your average copier sucks.

Sing lie, li lie, li lie, li lie lie lie lie, lie li lie li lie . . .
lie li lie, li lie li lie lie lie lie lie lie lie

Sing lie, li lie, li lie, li lie lie lie lie, lie li lie li lie . . .
lie li lie, li lie li lie lie lie lie lie lie lie

BALLADEER
Dance break!

(Dance break. Both BALLADEER and TRAGOS perform a "River-dance"-style Irish dance that is both accurate and ridiculous.)

(The music switches to just drums, the pace increases and creates an Irish "tribal" feel. The energy is contagious and the actors bodies represent the new "pace" of the performance.)

The day it finally happened,
the sky was red, not blue.

3M had trouble with a copier from 1962.

The office engineer gave up,
for he was far too weary.

He said, "I can do no more here!
It's time for Seamus O'Leary."

Seamus knew of this copier,
to his marrow he was chilled.

The secretaries sang songs
of all the temps that it had killed.

The copier was a beastly sight;
it filled the entire room.

It was shredding paper and belching fire
like a harbinger of doom.

Now Seamus was filled with fear,
but his job he would not shirk.

He said, "The Irish may not tan,
but Goddammit we can work."

Sing lili nacky hoogooga hickyhacky
nyack slappity boo!

Everybody!

(The BALLADEER prompts the audience to repeat the verse he has just sung.)

lili nacky hoogooga hickyhacky
nyack slappity boo!

(The TRAGOS now act out the scene that the BALLADEER is describing to the audience.)

He ripped open that copier,
a slave to foolish pride.

The wiring was faulty
and angry badgers lived inside.

Still Seamus pressed onward
because of the cut of his gib,

Inside he found a Twix bar
and six pints of Mr. Pibb.

The machine it whined and rumbled,
the screaming was quite shrill,

Then as quickly as it started—
everything was completely still.

(A drastic lighting change occurs to create a somber mood on stage. The music switches from a hard-driving drum beat to a traditional Irish lullaby. The TRAGOS switch from fast-paced frantic movements to slow and deliberate movements as the Balladeer sings the next verse.)

The workers approached quite slowly,
thinking maybe it was a trick.

They didn't run copies right away;
they just poked it with a stick.

Then Sandy pulled out a memo—
she was always quick on the draw.

She ran it through; the copy was true
and came out without a flaw.

The copy looked quite beautiful,
but it came at quite a cost,

For while the machine was fixed,
somewhere inside Seamus was lost.

But Seamus still lives on,
though his disappearance was quite heinous,

And they say when you see a smudge on your copy—
that's a little bit of Seamus.

Sing

(Music switches back to the beginning dance reel as actors perform a circular Irish dance that culminates with the audience clapping and the actors in a "traditional Riverdance" clog line ending with a final pose.)

lie, li lie, li lie, li lie lie lie lie, lie li lie li lie . . .
lie li lie, li lie li lie lie lie lie lie lie lie . . . Hey!

(Blackout.)

Explanation of the Secret

In order to create our products and to improvise, BNW staff and actors consistently utilize the skill of deferring judgment. If there is one thing our company has learned in over forty-five years of producing innovation, it is that at the beginning of the idea generation process, quantity is much more important than quality. As you will find when you read about our funnel process in chapter 10, we create approximately six hundred one-sentence ideas in order to produce the twenty-five sketches or songs that ultimately represent the finished product. We defer judgment completely during the first fifteen percent of our idea generation process in order to enable us to produce the bulk of ideas we need in order to "fill the pot."

Our ability to defer judgment on initial ideas is based on the understanding that we need *all* six hundred ideas in order to produce a few implementable ones. Many times the ideas we actually implement come as a result of combining or integrating several ideas created at the top of the funnel. These ideas sometimes bear little resemblance to the original idea.

As a group, we understand that early in the idea generation process our goal is not to come up with "the idea" but to come up with "an idea." This understanding allows us to rapidly produce mass quantities of ideas, and reduces the time constraints and fear involved in self-editing and judgment.

To encourage judgment deferment, we practice a recognition policy that rewards team members for the number of ideas they produce, not the quality of those ideas. Our goal is to become "idea machines." To increase the efficiency and production pace of those machines, the obstacle of judgment needs to be eliminated.

Another aspect to understanding judgment deferment is to trust that the process and hard realities of implementation will judge the idea and determine its validity. We recognize and are fully aware of the fact that all ideas will be judged and refined based on budget, physical plant restrictions, personnel abilities, marketability, and the like. Since these judgments are inevitable, we do not concern ourselves with that "given" at this point. We simply produce ideas regardless of how the idea may or may not ultimately work.

By treating judgment deferment almost as a policy, our team members, especially those who are motivated by doing things the "right way," feel comfortable learning and practicing a skill that is different and sometimes contrasting to typical or standard brainstorming practices. The policy of deferring judgment also helps individuals unlearn the seemingly automatic response of "what's wrong with that idea is . . ." or "the reason that won't work is . . ."

Because the accepted group standard is to defer judgment and because management clearly sets expectations that this is needed, an individual exhibiting judgment clearly stands out as someone who is not participating correctly in the process. This sort of group behavior observation and playful peer pressure creates an environment in which the only way an individual can screw up is to judge.

Another tool we use to maximize this part of the idea generation process, and therein the quality of our ultimate product, is to require the group to generate a set minimum number of ideas before they are allowed to move on to the next step. Over the years, we have determined that for the creation of our show scripts, that minimum number is six hundred ideas. This tactic prevents the group from worrying about the next step and allows them to focus solely on the task at hand—idea generation with reckless abandon.

Identifying the Corporate Need

When I think of deferring judgment in the corporate world, I instantly flash back to brainstorming sessions I was involved in as a corporate real estate consultant. The leader and facilitator began the session by letting everyone know the purpose of the session was to really "think outside the box." He or she asked everyone to let his or her hair down and think as nontraditionally as possible. The session then started and one of us spouted forth an idea— perhaps not a great idea, but one we thought was spontaneous, nontraditional and possibly even innovative. The facilitator would then stop the session and say something like, "Come on people, stop screwing around. We've got to focus—after all, this is a brainstorming session." At this point, I returned to doodling on my legal pad. In hindsight, it is no longer a mystery to me why these brainstorming sessions almost always produced the end result of "we should continue to do exactly what we're doing today with a 7% increase in sales and a 3% increase in market share."

Each of us has probably witnessed the classic example of how people's motivation to produce ideas can be extinguished. It usually goes something like this: the team leader says, "Okay, everybody let's be creative with our ideas." This is followed by an awkward three-to-five second pause in which people stare at each other, at the floor, or at the coffee stain on their shirt. You can almost hear "no, you go," "no, you go," then, finally, someone verbalizes an idea and it is immediately judged as "wrong." Think about what happens to the energy in the room. Are you shaking with excitement to come up with the next idea? Do the ideas seem to flow faster and easier, or is it painfully apparent that everyone in the brainstorming session is now reluctant to contribute?

Success Story: Education Minnesota

Like most states in the country, two separate unions represented the teachers in Minnesota schools. Although both unions had similar goals and practices, they each considered the other to be a competitor, or worse yet, an opponent. In an innovative decision that led other states to follow their lead, the two unions decided to merge. The Brave New Workshop agreed to facilitate the process of bringing the two unions together so the benefits of both could be integrated. The largest obstacle in doing so was to help both unions defer judgment and stop assuming the preconceived ideas they had about each other were true. We also wanted to help them see that, if given a chance, both sides could contribute to this new beginning. By exposing the union leaders to the secret of Deferring Judgment, we helped them move forward and successfully create a new, innovative organization. It was wonderful and rewarding to see individuals who previously viewed each other as competitors participate in improvisational exercises filled with laughter, collaboration, teamwork, and judgment deferment.

▲

"Brave New Workshop's creative approach to real world challenges was a critical assist in making the merger that established Education Minnesota a success. John's commitment and talent for using humor as a teaching tool was especially rewarding for two education unions. Fostering a new culture and getting beyond proud histories were vital steps in our journey. Deferring Judgment played a big role in successfully launching Education Minnesota."

Larry Wicks, Executive Director, Education Minnesota

The Secret of Deferring Judgment is Working When

- Brainstorming sessions no longer have the "I guess that's all the ideas we can think of" syndrome.
- There is more confidence in the voices of participants during brainstorming sessions.
- The volume of ideas is drastically increased.
- The body language of brainstorming participants displays excitement.
- Comments like "Is it already noon? Wow, we've been going at this for a couple of hours" become the norm.

- You and your team need more white board space.
- The ego portion of idea ownership is eliminated.
- Self-editing of the participants is eliminated, or at the very least, reduced.
- Increased diversity in the styles in which people feel comfortable presenting their ideas to the group is apparent.

The secret of Deferring Judgment is most effective in training sessions that deal with the subjects of leadership, teambuilding, and innovation.

BNW Product Application

I can offer hundreds of examples of how deferring judgment has benefited our idea generation process and enabled us to produce innovative products. There are literally dozens of ideas, concepts, and even fully developed sketches that were outrageously successful on our stage, despite my initial inclination toward thinking they were a "bad" idea. The *Ballad of Seamus O'Leary,* which is the script example at the beginning of this chapter, perhaps exemplifies how deferring judgment enables ideas to become more than what you initially think they are. It also demonstrates how deferring judgment at the beginning of the process can allow ideas to affect each other and create a new idea that, in this case, was unbelievably exceptional.

The theme for the show we were writing was "humor in the workplace." During the idea sharing portion of our process, one of the actors declared, "The most important job in the world is copy repair person." That idea was added to our list of six hundred on the Master Inspiration List we refer to in chapter 10. Later in the brainstorming session, another actor declared, "I hate *Riverdance.*" In a more typical workplace setting, perhaps someone in the group—or even the leader—may have said, "What does *Riverdance* have to do with the workplace?" or "That's funny, unfortunately, none of us know how to dance," or "We don't have a budget for clogs," or "I'm not comfortable keeping my arms that straight." In adhering to the BNW creative funnel process, we immediately added the *Riverdance* idea to the list without question, comment, or judgment. As those two ideas traveled down through our creative process, they eventually and organically met and combined. The newly formed idea was then expanded and refined. Ultimately, the end product was a fully choreographed song, specifically a *Riverdance* parody that told the story of a third-generation, Irish, immigrant copy repairman named Seamus O'Leary. The piece closed the first act of the show and received a standing ovation many times as we went into intermission—a true rarity in theatre. Thank *goodness* we defer judgment at the Brave New Workshop.

BNW Management Application

A few years ago, I volunteered our actors to participate in a local festival as interactive characters. The actors were expected to simply walk throughout the festival in costume, create conversation and improvise humor as a way to reinforce the theme of the event. In turn, we were given a trade show booth to promote our shows. As BNW team members were brainstorming ideas on how to maximize the benefit of our trade show booth, one of our employees suggested that we should provide festival attendees the opportunity to purchase tickets at our booth. Having a considerable amount of past experience with trade shows, I initially judged the idea based on the fact that most people simply walk by the booth, grab some literature, and move on. I felt that very few people were likely to investigate a particular show date and time and then buy a ticket at the booth. Since we were in the first fifteen percent of our brainstorming process, I decided to defer judgment. As the idea was expanded and affected by the other team members it became clear that my perception was narrow and uninformed. The team said yes to the idea and created a trade show booth experience complete with an interactive game—a game so popular it caused a traffic problem at the trade show. We sold more tickets to our shows during the sixteen hours of the trade show than we typically sold in three weeks. Often, surprisingly successful results seem to occur when, as a company, we aggressively implement the secret of Deferring Judgment. Here are some words from one of our employees as to how she sees deferring judgment in our workplace.

From Our Employees

The area where I see the biggest difference between the Brave New Workshop and other organizations is this concept of deferring judgment, when working together to solve problems or generate ideas. I can't recall anywhere else I've ever worked that effectively says "yes, first" to all ideas, or treats all ideas equally in the initial stages, the way we do—even though I've worked in environments where a lot of lip service is paid to this notion!

It's so much a part of the way we work around here, it's an unconscious response. So now, when I go to a brainstorming meeting with another association or organization, I'm always surprised to see how people start throwing up limitations and blocking ideas right at the beginning of the process. The rationale seems to be, why waste time talking about it if it's not what we're looking for?

Now, I see it just the opposite way. For instance, maybe someone suggests that it would be beneficial for us to participate in this trade show, or promote our shows at an event that doesn't at first seem like a natural fit for us. Rather than bringing up all the reasons why it won't work, or that we don't have the right resources, we all say yes and support the idea. And what's the worst-case scenario? We see the idea all the way through, and we don't get good results; it's a flop. But even in that case, look at the valuable information we gain. Look at how much more experience we bring the next time a similar opportunity comes up!

But more often than not, the idea exceeds everyone's expectations. I observe it all the time around here—we're constantly accomplishing things that technically, "we don't have the money or the skills or the manpower" to do. We find a way to make it work, and I think it's not because we're geniuses or magicians—that's just the fruits of not shooting ideas down right away.

Erin Farmer, Director of Group Sales

SECRET 3

Sharing Focus & Accepting All Styles

BRAVE NEW WORKSHOP THEATRE

DATE: 08.23.00

SHOW: Dull Man Running, or the
Bush Little Gore House in Texas

TITLE: "Tiger!"

DRAFT: FINAL

PREMISE:
Clueless suburban school board member reveals her ignorance and racist beliefs in an emotional testimony regarding an urban exchange with a Minneapolis high school.

SETTING:
School Board meeting at Apple Valley Middle School library in Apple Valley, a typical, mostly white, modern-day "Leave It to Beaver"-type suburb.

CHARACTERS:
SUSAN PLUNKETT: A young white woman who fancies herself a liberal minded intellectual. Susan sells Pampered Chef and has tons of friends who look like her. Married with three kids.

MORTON GRAZER: School Board President. Fifty-three years old, white, married with two kids in college. Morton has lived in Apple Valley for twenty-five years. Morton has a comb-over.

JAN NELSON: School Board member for twelve years. She's a retired gym teacher.

Various school board members.

(Lights up on school board meeting.)

MORTON

Alrightee then! It looks like the teacher's lounge will get a
new microwave. I'll inform the Apple Valley Lounge Boosters to
move forward on that one. *(Shifts uncomfortably.)* Now . . . it seems
that, uh, we have one more action item on our list today and, uh,
I think we all know how we feel about this one. Yeah, this action
item is real different. It's been proposed that the Apple Valley
school district—that's us!—do an *(Starts reading from notes.)*
urban exchange with some schools over there in Minneapolis.
So, okay, let's vote! All opposed—

JAN

(Suspiciously.) Whoa, I'm sorry. What is an
"urban exchange" exactly?

MORTON

Yes, that's a good question, Jan. Real helpful. *(Reading from notes.)*
"An urban exchange will challenge suburban and metropolitan
schools alike to participate in a learning operative meant to
bridge cultural and educational differences along diverse lines
of color, race, and creed."

(Silence.)

JAN

Okay, I'm confused. What is this, Morton? You said "exchange"
in there somewhere. What are we exchanging?

MORTON

Uh . . . students, Jan, students.

JAN

Exchange them for what?

MORTON

Other students.

JAN

Students from Minneapolis?

MORTON

Yes!

JAN

(Getting it.) Oh my God!

MORTON

(Reading.) Students from Minneapolis North, Roosevelt—that's where Governor Ventura went I might add *(No response from board.)* . . . So, any discussion . . . *(As if expecting.)* Susan?

SUSAN

(Already standing—seems surprised that she's been called on so quickly.) Oh, well! Good! Here I am! *(Pause.)* Well, this is exciting. Don't you think? Yes, very exciting and different. Minneapolis schools are very rich in diversity and that's a good thing. I am not one of those racist people. I am not a racist. In fact, I love black people. I really, really do. I love that Tiger Woods. I think he is just so . . . wonderful and . . . just wonderful. *(Starts getting revved up.)* I'd invite him in my home, that's how wonderful I think he is. I wish he were mine. I would trade one of my own sons for Tiger—that's how much I love black people! Let's just say, I'm comfortable with them, with those people . . . All people! . . . I don't even notice color. I'm color-blind, really. Color-blind! All I see is white! I watch Oprah every day and I forget she's black. Absolutely forget! And that Halle Berry, you know her right? An African-American actress—so beautiful. I mean, she looks white! I would love to be as pretty as Halle Berry. And that Tiger is just so wonderful, too.

(Susan sits. Silence. Scattered claps.)

MORTON

Thank you, Susan. Okay, so, just to clarify, you are in favor of inner city kids coming to our school?

SUSAN

Oh, no! No!

(Blackout or transition.)

Explanation of the Secret

Because the actors of the Brave New Workshop are also improvisers, they have an inherent ability to share focus with each other on stage. As an improv scene progresses the actors organically decide to react in a way that gives the appropriate person the proper amount of focus at any given time during the scene. They change their position on stage so that the person speaking can be most clearly seen by the audience and create a seamless "give and take" in their dialogue to ensure that two people are not speaking at the same time. To the audience it appears as if they have a set discipline or that the scene is in fact scripted and rehearsed. The truth is they are simply respectful of each other's need for focus and put the success of the scene ahead of their own need to have their idea heard. Unlike stand up comedy, improvisation actually rewards the performers for a sense of egoless cooperation.

Improvisers also understand that respecting drastically different styles is a way to add depth and dimension to the scene. Two characters with significantly different points of view and styles can create a much more richly entertaining scene than two similar characters. There are countless examples of this in well-known comedies, for example Archie Bunker and Meathead in *All in the Family*, Frank Burns and Hawkeye in *M.A.S.H.*, Kramer and Jerry in *Seinfeld*, or Lisa and Bart Simpson in *The Simpsons*.

By accepting another person's unique style you also show them they have your endorsement to be their most unique and original self. We found this empowerment leads people to blossom and increases their confidence and productivity. We also observed that an ensemble made up of a diverse cast of characters produces products that are always more innovative than a group of similar styles.

Accepting someone's style could be as easy as allowing them to communicate in the way in which they are most comfortable. Some people prefer written communication, and others prefer to communicate verbally. Some people are more comfortable sharing their ideas one-on-one; others like the group dynamic.

Because our goal is to encourage and facilitate everyone to become their most original and unique self, it is vital that we allow them to add to the process in their own way. We found that the number of ideas a person can generate is directly related to his or her ability to communicate those ideas in a style in which they are most confident.

At first, many people think our concept of sharing focus means making sure that each individual gets their fifteen minutes on stage or that everyone gets equal time to communicate their ideas within our creative process. This assumes everyone has similar needs and comfort levels with having the focus on him or her. However some individuals actually feel uncomfortable being in the spotlight. We must give them the opportunity to share their ideas in the time they need and through the vehicle that works best for them. We have learned that for many, sharing ideas is a risk—especially if emotional consequences are attached to their sharing. If someone is fearful of the idea sharing process, we work to create a mechanism that best suits his or her personality and style.

This does not mean that some individuals are not expected to contribute as much as others. Everyone is still responsible for equal portions of idea generation—they are just allowed to meet their idea quota in a manner that maximizes their own preferred style of contribution.

In encouraging people to share ideas and focus in their own way, we have, time after time, found wonderful solutions in the ideas these non-traditional team members generate. Our shows have greatly benefited from some outlandish and innovative ideas that were a direct result of the manner in which these non-conforming ideas were communicated to the rest of the team. The communication vehicle itself oftentimes was so unusual that it ended up in the show too.

During the writing process of one of our holiday shows, one

of the actresses thought she could best communicate her idea by drawing kindergarten style images with crayons on a piece of cardboard. That communication style ultimately inspired a sketch, which featured a young foreign exchange student using crayon drawings to satirize her perception of the "American Christmas."

Identifying the Corporate Need

In some work environments, individuals are asked to contribute ideas with the mandate of how those ideas must be generated and communicated to the team. Little emphasis is placed on allowing people to brainstorm in their own style or offering team members the ability to control how much focus and attention they receive. For example, if the team leader is an extrovert who enjoys the group process and likes to use verbal skills and high-energy practices to create ideas, people in the group who are less verbal may become uncomfortable and withdraw from the idea generation process.

What if you were in a meeting brainstorming the next great direct mail piece for your new product launch campaign? The team leader asks everyone to quickly draw on the white board a rough sketch of some of their ideas. You freeze. You do not have a lick of artistic training, and you couldn't trace a circle around an upside down coffee cup. How comfortable, successful, and productive do you think you'll be in sharing that great idea bouncing around in your mind's eye? What if, instead, the team leader gave you a week to share your idea and suggested that you can use your art department to help you with the mock up? Ah, time and talent at your disposal—what a treat! If that leader allowed each member of the team to generate an idea in their own style, he or she would have a greater quantity, and ultimately better quality, of ideas to choose from.

Unfortunately, some individuals who are full of wonderful and innovative ideas may be viewed as sullen, non-participating appendages, disconnected or, worse yet, lazy. Perhaps the real truth is that they are being asked to create ideas (already an emotional risk) in a way that is not suited for their style or comfort with focus. A drastic example of this sort of misclassification is Albert Einstein, who was labeled by many as lazy and arrogant by traditional academic standards of the time because he preferred a process of discovery and innovation that was isolated and introspective.

One way of accommodating the different needs of the group is to continually change and vary the types of styles and focus levels you use. We found that if team members understand that the team will be using a series of vehicles to create ideas, they work harder to produce ideas even in a style that makes them uncomfortable. They look forward to the next style, which may be better suited to their needs. Varying the way you approach idea generation is a wonderful way to show respect for all the different styles, personalities, and individual comfort levels that exist in your group. If you are unable to respond to individual communication style needs, you risk the possibility of receiving fewer ideas and equally, fewer opportunities for innovation.

Success Story: General Mills / Yoplait Division

The Yoplait Division of General Mills is considered to be one of the most creative and innovative groups of people within General Mills and, for that matter, the industry. This group had just created, marketed, and distributed one of their most successful products ever, Go-Gurt. This product was innovative in every way, its ingredients, its packaging, and its marketing. It was a home run. As the division planned for their annual marketing meeting, they had a unique yet undeniable need. They needed to find a way to keep the level of their creativity and innovation at least at its current level as they embarked on the challenge of finding the next Go-Gurt. This need was compounded by the fact that because of their success, the division was growing and had been infused with new team members. Some of these newbies were much younger and less experienced than the existing leadership. This diversity caused a natural increase in the type of styles and scope of ideas that the group generated. One of the newer members of the team was quoted as saying that he felt like he had just been chosen to join the New York Yankees a day after they had won the World Series. The Brave New Workshop interviewed several team members from varying levels of experience. We also researched the dynamics of the culture that was in place at the time of the Go-Gurt idea generation. The goal was to understand what worked and to create a system that would ensure continued creativity and innovation at that level. The Brave New Workshop spent the day with this group in the beautiful surroundings of the Minnesota Northwoods. The group was led through a series of improvisational exercises that reinforced the elements needed in a creative work environment and allowed individuals who had not yet worked together to create and share ideas in a safe and non-threatening environment. The results were immediately evident. The interactive nature of the improvisational workshop was a perfect way to get individuals with different levels of experience and different styles of creativity to work together. It also reinforced to the group that perhaps the most important aspect of creative culture is the ability to accept new ideas. They were all reminded of the level of acceptance it took to embrace Go-Gurt in its initial stages of creation. Many of the group also commented on the impact of being reminded creativity and innovation are skills that need to be maintained and nurtured. They were ready to produce the next home run.

"The Brave New Workshop component of our Yoplait 'off-site' was incredibly well received. People thought it was really fun, and, more importantly, took away a lot from it.

"You guys definitely did a great job on all fronts—just incorporating enough about Yoplait. People thought it was great that you got a pulse on what was going on in the division and also had some unique ways to bring the more academic organizational behavior things to life in a much more relevant way than they had seen before.

"So, great work! I wouldn't hesitate to call you again."

Steve Young, Promotions Manager, Yoplait/Colombo Division

The Secret of Sharing Focus and Accepting All Styles is Working When

- Individual team members develop a positive reputation for the type and styles they create. You will hear things like, "oh, that idea sounds just like Mary."
- You start to hear comments like, "I never knew that about you," or "wow, that's a cool way of looking at things."
- Employees who once seemed timid are now proactive and aggressive in their desire to contribute.
- Employees believe they are valued because of their individual characteristics and not for their ability to conform to the status quo of the company.
- The number of bullet point memorandums reduces dramatically.
- There is an increased sense of employee loyalty.

The secret of Sharing Focus and Accepting All Styles is most effective in training sessions that focus on diversity and team-building.

BNW Product Application

When we began creating and rehearsing the show *Don't Smell the Sweaty Stuff, or A Chicken's Soup for the Passive Aggressive Soul*, it became apparent that our group was not well versed in the individual styles of the other team members because they had not previously worked with each other. To assist the process, we asked each team member to take some time to think about whom their favorite comedic actors were and what type of comedy they enjoyed the most. When the group shared their perspectives with each other, we heard things one would expect comedic actors to bring up: Woody Allen, Mel Brooks, the Marx Brothers, *South Park*, and the like. Then it was time for a new cast member to share his perspective on what type of comedy he liked. He said simply, "I love chimp films." When we pushed him for a deeper understanding, we found out that not only did he literally like comedy movies that featured chimp actors, but he was more comfortable on stage portraying a chimp than a human being. Adhering to our practice of allowing people to find their optimal level of focus and style, we eventually wrote a hilarious parody of *Inside the Actors Studio* in which the actor being interviewed was a chimp. This sketch enabled our actor to perform a character he was passionate about to rave reviews. It also added significantly to the show's variety and clearly made the satirical point that perhaps Hollywood actors take themselves a bit too seriously.

BNW Management Application

The Brave New Workshop aggressively pursues individuals who have drastically different personality styles and levels of comfort with being the center of attention. It is our way of ensuring the product we produce will have as many distinct points of view as possible and be accessible to the diverse styles and points of view of our audiences. Many assume most comedic actors and writers are extroverts and enjoy receiving attention and focus. In my experience, I haven't found this to be true. A large percentage of BNW writers are actually very uncomfortable with attention and would most likely be considered dark and brooding introverts by the majority of society. We have people who perform comedy for a living, yet would much prefer to create ideas by jotting them down in a notebook instead of verbally brainstorming. In any given cast, we have individuals who are interested in political satire, others who are passionate about physical comedy, some who love to sing, others who love to tell jokes, and yes, some who have a passion for chimps. We have writers who approach idea generation through the eyes of the character, some who need to improvise on stage to get a feel for where the sketch is going, and still others who rely on their bodies to help create unusual ideas and actions. We have idea generators who need to remove themselves from the group process from time to time and let ideas percolate in solitude over a mix of wheat germ and cigarettes. We value them all equally, and we're thankful they continue to safely create in their own unique style.

Throughout the idea generation process we adhere to sharing focus appropriately so ideas are generated and refined in several ways. By making our team members comfortable with idea sharing, we ensure that each individual is operating at his or her most productive level. Purely and simply, we believe the diversity of styles is directly related to the quality of our product.

From Our Employees

> When I first started, I was hired as the theatre manager, which was sort of a glorified scheduler/cleaner/concession-stand-worker position at the time. As I got more involved in the company and learned more about the need for us to focus (as a company) on our corporate entertainment and training division, I started talking with (well, "lobbying" is actually a better word) Dawn, BNW Director of Marketing, to let me take on her theatre marketing responsibilities

so she could dedicate more time to the corporate services marketing.

In retrospect, I am amazed that she was so open to the idea because here I was, a new kid with no graphic design training and minimal marketing experience, trying to hone in on her turf and essentially take over her job!!! But amazingly she just shared focus with me, let me grow into the position and shifted her own position towards the more profitable corporate marketing.

Although she has admitted that secretly it was emotionally hard to pass off some of her job to me, the collaboration between us has been fun and productive, and our corporate product marketing efforts were finally able to explode! I think this is an amazing example of Dawn saying yes to my idea AND being willing to share focus when most people would have told me to go take a flying leap. Pretty rad.

Julia DeRuyter, Director of Theatre Marketing and Management

Not to sound like a pompous jerk, but I am the kind of person who never had to worry about the acceptance of different styles. I am that annoying person who likes to express herself verbally, in writing, on the phone, in an email, or even through shockingly bad drawings. In my experience as a writer/performer at the BNW, I have always been fairly confident in expressing my ideas, so you would think that this point doesn't really pertain to me, but it does. I always hated working in groups. Hated it! I hated it because there was always that one person who didn't do anything, and because every member of the group was going to be evaluated on the product we created, the rest of us had to pick up the slack. You know that guy. You may have been that guy. Now, you would think that when five people with different levels of experience, different ages, and vastly different styles of communicating ideas get together to try to create a cohesive two-hour show it would be a nightmare, especially for an anal-retentive people pleaser who has been accused of being a smarty-pants. (That would be me.) But, miraculously, that has never been the case. And believe me, I have worked with some extremely "creative" minds (read: people incapable of writing a sentence, tying their shoes, or washing their pants). When we all express ourselves in our own way, we find ourselves making the ideas work. The newness and novelty of an idea in a form that would never have occurred to me spurs me on to help make that idea a reality. So, when somebody brings in an idea that can only be expressed on the back of an orange rind, I find myself drawn to use my skills to help make it concrete. And because of this cooperation, I have often found myself a part of something far more creative and interesting than I could have ever come up with on my own. So who's the smarty-pants, now?

Katy McEwen, Actor, Director, Instructor

Declarations

BRAVE NEW WORKSHOP THEATRE

DATE: 1.18.01

SHOW: How to Try in Business Without Really Succeeding, or A Cubicle Named Desire

TITLE: "You're Fired!"

DRAFT: FINAL

PREMISE:
In an attempt to prevent a messy lawsuit, a boss goes to ridiculous lengths to fire his employee without actually saying the words "You're fired!"

SETTING:
George Harrison's roomy office with two doors and wood paneling trim.

CHARACTERS:
GEORGE HARRISON: George's behind is on the line because his team's numbers are down this month. George has been told by "The Powers That Be" to fire Bob, but to do so in a way that saves the company from the nuisance of a lawsuit.

BOB THOMAS: Bob has been with the company for two years. Bob just doesn't get that he's incompetent.

(Lights up on GEORGE and BOB in GEORGE's office. They have been here a long time and the feeling in the room is heavy and confused. GEORGE has a puppet on his hand.)

GEORGE

(In puppet voice and tune of "Retail" song.) Somebody has to go!
And his name is Bob! Somebody has to go!

BOB

(A bit frightened.) I'm—I'm sorry, Mr. Harrison. I still don't get it.

GEORGE

(In puppet voice.) That's okay, Bob!
Maybe I didn't explain it right!

BOB

Yes, maybe that's it.

GEORGE

(Pulling puppet off his hand dejectedly.) Well, Bob,
maybe a story will help to illustrate my point.

BOB

Yes, Mr. Harrison.

GEORGE

Yes, yes, indeed, Bob. A story. *(Big sigh.)* This is a story about a
guy named . . . Gob . . . Yes, Gob. And Gob was an employee at
the magical kingdom of . . . 4M! Everyone liked Gob a great deal,
but one day it became apparent that Gob's output had decreased
by 50 percent. Gob's boss Mr. Harrison—Ford-ibon realized that
if Gob didn't go far, far away—and soon—he would lose a lot of
money as well as his job and probably his second wife—but no
one at the 4M kingdom wanted the lawsuit fairies to come. Oh,
God no, Gob! So, bibbidee-bobbidee-boo, Gob lived happily ever
after, but he was far, far away. God Bless Us Everyone
and The End.

BOB

(Confused.) I'm sorry. What are you trying to say Mr. Harrison?

GEORGE

Yes, yes, good question, Gob. Let's see here.
(Flips off lights and picks up remote.) Here are some pictures
that might help you to understand.

BOB

O-O-Okay.

GEORGE

(Flipping to picture of office building.)
Here's where we work.

BOB

Okay.

GEORGE

(Flipping to picture of demolished building.) And here's what
will happen if you continue to work here.

BOB

Is this because I don't turn my computer off at night?

GEORGE

(Impatient.) Okay, let's try this. *(Flipping to picture of BOB at desk.)*
Here's you at your desk. *(Flipping to picture of BOB'S desk with
Melanie sitting at it and waving.)* Okay—and here's your desk
next Monday morning at 8:00 A.M.

BOB

What is Melanie doing at my desk?
Are you moving me to another office?

GEORGE

Jesus, Gob! *(Slightly hysterical.)* This is you! *(Flipping to
stick figure of BOB with "Bob" written underneath.)*

BOB

Okay.

(GEORGE flips to picture of BOB'S stick figure in flames.)

BOB

Why am I on fire? Wait—am I fired? Are you firing me?

(GEORGE flips to "YES!!")

GEORGE

(with puppet) Bye-bye, Gob!

(Blackout or transition.)

Explanation of the Secret

Many improvisers feel the first five seconds are the most important part of an improv scene. In those five seconds the impetus for the scene is born, and the chain reaction of declaration—reaction—action is started. Ensemble improvisation requires participants to constantly gather information from each other and instantaneously create something from nothing. Declaring your point of view is not only polite, it is vital in helping your fellow improvisers understand "what your deal is." It gives them clear understanding of whom you are so they can discover who they are.

At the Brave New Workshop, we ask our improvisers to declare their point of view loudly, clearly, and quickly. We recognize this declaration is the foundation needed to build the scene. If two improvisers begin a scene with clearly stated points of view, then the scene can simply and organically focus on the two points of view working together to create the action of the scene while sharing space and time. It is a beautiful and clear representation of perfect collaboration.

If the declaration is not clear at the beginning of a scene, the scene tends to hobble along without much progress. The audience may notice that the improvisers seem to have a tint of confusion in everything they do. Declarations build clarity, which lead to confidence and purpose in an improvisational scene. Sometimes it feels as if the declarations at the top of a scene are like marching papers. When an improviser understands his or her own point of view, and the point of view of his or her fellow improvisers, the scene seems easier to navigate and almost writes itself. There are many classic examples of this in well-known comedy. We, as viewers, didn't care what Sam and Diane from *Cheers* were doing, as long as they were doing it while sticking to their identifiable points of view. Each of the *Three Stooges* had a very clear and identifiable point of view. It didn't matter to us whether or not they were painting a house or stopping a bank robbery or going fishing, we just wanted to see them stick to their points of view and interact with each other.

In Minnesota, we suffer from what is referred to as "Minnesota

Nice," and part of our culture believes that clearly and loudly declaring your point of view is a sign of arrogance or inappropriate outspokenness. Some people have a tendency to never let anyone else know how they truly feel. This is death for an improvisation scene. I refer to it as the Minnesota Norwegian Lutheran Verbal Square Dance. The truth is, at least in an improv scene, the nicest or most polite thing you can do is to confidently declare your point of view at the top of the scene.

I believe that declaring your point of view early and strongly can be applied to any situation in which groups are trying to evaluate a challenge and find a solution. Clear declarations at the beginning of a project significantly add to the quality of the solution. If a person decides to withhold their point of view, or otherwise useful information, until later in the discussion, the group must "back track" in order to incorporate the new information into generating a solution and affecting the outcome.

Keep in mind our secret of Sharing Focus and Accepting All Styles *(chapter 3)*. This concept has a direct application to making declarations. Individuals must be able to declare their point of view in the style and communication vehicle that works best for them. However, the individual is responsible for contributing to the process and supporting the group by ensuring he or she declares their point of view.

Identifying the Corporate Need

The issue of declarations shows itself in the corporate world in what many people refer to as "the meeting after the meeting." It goes something like this: groups of people are asked to come together to analyze the situation, create a plan, and find a solution. The facilitator of the meeting genuinely wants everyone's input and point of view. He or she has developed innovative ways to allow people to share ideas and has been sensitive to the different styles and comfort levels of the people on the team. After receiving less information than expected, the facilitator finally says, "Does anyone else have anything to say? Is there anything else someone would like to share? We need to make sure we get everyone's point of view before we move forward. Anyone? Anyone?" The facilitator is met with silence. Members of the group twiddle their pencils and awkwardly look around the room. The meeting is adjourned. Immediately, and sometimes almost in a panic, members of the group retreat to their secret communication caves, which take the form of restrooms, smoke break rooms and copy rooms. They huddle together in smaller groups and say things like, "Well, I'll tell you what I think . . . ," or "If someone ever asks me my opinion . . . ," or "I was just about to say . . ." It is obviously a bit late for declarations as the content of these "meetings after the meeting" are not shared with the rest of the group or the facilitator. Unfortunately, these post-meeting declarations will not help the group to find the best solution. C'mon folks, just say what you have to say when someone can actually use the information.

The other observation I see regarding declarations is an all too common situation in which an organizational leader asks a team to execute a project and then somewhere, usually near the end of a project, the leader infuses new expectations. Unfortunately, the group has spent a considerable amount of time and effort creating a solution independent of the leader's new expectations because they didn't know the expectations even existed. The entire team was under the assumption they were empowered to create a solution solely on their own points of view. With new information from the leader, the group is pressured to inorganically incorporate what the leader wants. Boy, oh boy, does that tick people off!

Success Story: Carlson School of Management, University of Minnesota

Declarations do not have to be huge, opinionated, earth-shattering announcements. They can simply be the conscious choice to share what you know with other members of the team without worrying about being right or wrong. This can be a difficult skill for new leaders to practice and learn, especially those who might lack confidence in an unfamiliar business setting such as a recent college graduate. The Carlson School of Management at the University of Minnesota is tasked with identifying the skills that employers are looking for in newly minted MBAs and then working with the students to prepare them to compete in a highly competitive marketplace. In visits with national employers, the instructors continually heard that leadership was the single most important piece of the MBA "package" besides academic success. This resulted in a comprehensive leadership initiative at the Carlson School that led to the belief two key ingredients of leadership are self-confidence and the ability to declare your point of view. Working closely with the Director of the Carlson School of Management, the Brave New Workshop presented an academic training session that focused on teaching the students how to be confident in thinking on their feet in a variety of business scenarios and then openly expressing themselves. In a few hours time, the students moved from an unresponsive audience to an actively participating, engaged group. More than half of the students volunteered to participate in the exercises. They were energetic and excited about finding a step-by-step way to prepare for difficult, challenging situations. They never considered the fact that they could prepare ahead and that, indeed, they actually had all the tools needed to declare themselves appropriately and confidently in the fast-paced world of business.

▲

"The student response to John's workshop was overwhelmingly positive. Comments included: 'You should conduct this workshop more often;' 'I came away with the skills that I need to be a more effective leader. All I need to do is practice them.' 'The best part of Boot Camp was the Brave New Workshop guy.' 'I enjoyed learning the confidence techniques from the Brave New Workshop.' 'Brave New Workshop—Outstanding.'

"Because this was so successful, we are hoping to work with John to develop a regular improv 'class' here at Carlson. This will give the students ongoing opportunities to practice and hone their skills. We want them to hit the ground running when they start their new jobs."

Clare Foley, Director Graduate Business Career Center
Carlson School of Management, Full-Time MBA Program
University of Minnesota

The Secret of Declarations is Working When

- Direct and honest communication between team members and leaders is common.
- Individual knowledge between team members is increasingly shared.
- Results begin to clearly reflect a more diverse point of view.
- Fewer employees complain that their ideas have not been heard.

The secret of Declarations seems most apparent in training sessions that deal with the subjects of innovation and communication.

BNW Product Application

Declarations play a big part in forming the exposition at the top of a scene in our scripted products. Because we perform in a rather minimalist type of theatre, we do not have the luxury of communicating information via extravagant sets, costumes, or technological devices. Over the years this lack of theatrical accoutrement encouraged us to be incredibly declarative and clear at the beginning of a sketch or song. Typically we try to let the audience know who we are, where we are, what our point of view is, and what we are trying to accomplish in a scene within the first thirty seconds of the sketch. We found that if we provide the audience with clear information at the top of a scene, they spend more time enjoying the rest of the scene instead of trying to figure out what exactly is going on. Of course, there are instances in which we purposely confuse the audience or make them feel uncomfortable as a comedic device, but these are separate from declarations. Our goal is to bring clarity to the scene right from the start so the audience can sit back, laugh, and enjoy the experience without the burden of confusion.

BNW Management Application

As owners of the Brave New Workshop and leaders of our group, my wife, Jenni, and I work daily to create a workplace that allows our employees to feel creatively safe and we take full responsibility for making it work. We fully expect all of our employees to take responsibility for declaring their point of view, their needs, and their opinions. We actually have very little tolerance for individuals who choose not to be forthright with their declarations. Again, we can only take this position because we are confident we have created an environment in which employees know their declarations are welcomed and respected.

We view withholding a point of view as an active choice and as an infringement on our policy for respecting fellow teammates. Remember, we run our company like an improv scene; therefore, when someone chooses not to declare their point of view, it makes it extremely difficult, and sometimes impossible, for other team members to improvise and work with that person. Similarly, we believe that in many ways *not* declaring your point of view can be construed as being dishonest, simply because not fully disclosing ideas that could ultimately help the team steals time, energy, and a potentially better outcome.

This may seem to be a harsh standard to impose on employees

who are introverted or shy. Remember, that in adhering to our philosophy of sharing focus and accepting all styles, those employees are given endless opportunities to declare their point of view in whatever manner works for them. We don't care how they declare, just as long as they do.

From Our Employees

The single biggest reason I agreed to join the Brave New Workshop as the Director of Corporate Services in February 2003 was the promise of a work environment free of drama. At the time, the Corporate Services division was in a state of disarray, the salary being offered was less than what I was making at my current position and the office space was not exactly "glamorous." John Sweeney kept telling me, "The biggest reason you should come to work here is that I can guarantee you that you will love the work environment. Period." He was right.

What John didn't know is that I pulled several of his current employees aside (many of whom I already knew through business connections) to "test the waters" and see if what he was telling me was true. To my astonishment, they all told the same story, but it was nearly too good to be true. I thought to myself, "C'mon, this is a theatre, there has to be some drama!"

All of the BNW employees I spoke to unequivocally stated that there was an established culture of honest and direct communication. They viewed this culture as the key to their happiness with their jobs. It was explained to me that everyone worked productively and respectfully because most thoughts and ideas regarding the direction of the company were shared in an open forum. Passive aggressive behavior or "drama" amongst the staff members was not tolerated. Anyone who was not able to buy into this culture of direct communication was simply asked to leave.

As explained earlier in this chapter, there is a difference between declaring your point of view and aggressive, disruptive behavior. The bottom line is that if you have an idea, problem, concern, or worry at the Brave New Workshop, you are expected to share this with others and know that you will be rewarded for having declared your point of view. If your natural tendency is to internalize these feelings and act out negatively because of them, you will not fit in because the established culture does not tolerate this behavior. There should be a sign in the window at the Workshop that states, "DRAMA QUEENS NEED NOT APPLY."

What John and Jenni have created is a staff of highly functional individuals who believe that life is too short for there to be cliques and drama within the workplace. It gets in the way of productivity and profitability. Why waste so much time and emotional energy with infighting when you could be out there making money? We just declare and move forward with the process of making the world a better place through laughter and improvisation. Life is too short, and we spend too much time working for there to be drama.

I now operate under virtually one rule: Declare your point of view early and often. It's the most respectful thing you can do.

Troy Alexander, Director of Corporate Services

When I first began working for the Brave New Workshop in March, 2003, I had expressed great interest in exercising a flexible work schedule to allow me to be able to work from home semi-regularly. In the first weeks, this worked wonderfully for me because I had not been assigned a designated office space at the theater, and the team members with whom I worked closely were often in and out as well.

My schedule was never the same two weeks in a row, and the lines between when I was "working from home" and just "at home, but not technically working" quickly began to blur. My project work began spilling over into evenings and weekends, and I felt the need to be responsive because it seemed as though everyone else was working during these "off" hours as well.

Over time, it became apparent that this haphazard work schedule was a bit too unstructured for me, and I needed to reintroduce some boundaries in order to reclaim some much-needed personal time. I struggled with doing this for some time, as I feared it would make me seem selfish or worse—not dedicated enough. I continued to disrespect the time of each day that should've been set aside for personal or family time, out of fear that making a declaration about needing to change this would be ill-received.

I couldn't have been more wrong.

On the phone with our president, John Sweeney, I declared that I needed to more clearly define my work schedule but maintain some flexibility each week in order to be happier in my position. Not only was my declaration quickly acknowledged and embraced, but it felt as if a fifty-pound weight had been lifted from my shoulders.

Now I regularly declare my weekly schedule to both John and to my family, so that everyone knows exactly where I'll be and what my availability is at any time on any given day—and they can all make sure I'm sticking to it! This simple action has allowed me to be happier, because I have reclaimed my personal time, and more productive because I've committed to working hard during the hours I've scheduled. It seems like a very small step, but it's been a small step with huge results—all because I declared my need to change something about the way I was working.

Today, I've found that it's much easier (and fun!) to declare my point-of-view about things, because of the sentiment of acceptance that's present around me every day.

Jen Bellmont, Associate Producer Corporate Services

Create a Statusless Environment

BRAVE NEW WORKSHOP THEATRE

DATE: 08.23.00

SHOW: Dull Man Running, or the
Bush Little Gore House in Texas

TITLE: "Delaware"

DRAFT: FINAL

PREMISE:
Washington questions his abilities as a leader while crossing the
Delaware. A young soldier reassures him, but reveals a number of
the general's faults in the process.

SETTING:
A rowboat crossing the Delaware river towards Trenton, New
Jersey. It is before sunrise on December 25th, 1776. It is freezing.

CHARACTERS:
WASHINGTON: Our first president. A general who is not sure
about whether or not he is ready to lead. Also, a despicable
human being in many respects.

ELLIOT: A sixteen year old who lied about his age so he could en-
list in the army. He worships the ground Washington walks on.

SAM: Just some guy rowing a boat for atmosphere.

*(We hear "Silent Night" softly playing and the sound of oars cutting
through the water. Lights up. WASHINGTON posed in the bow of a boat.
ELLIOT and SAM are rowing. WASHINGTON sighs audibly.)*

ELLIOT

What's wrong, General Washington?

WASHINGTON

Oooh, it's just that it's Christmas, Elliot. You know how
every year during the holidays you look back over your
life and evaluate where you are? Well, it's Christmas and
here I am crossing the Delaware. If we win this battle, it
could be the turning point of the war, and then everybody
is going to look to me for leadership. I'm just not sure I'm
ready to lead a new country.

ELLIOT

Well, if it's any consolation, sir, I think a toothless, slave owning,
hemp farmer who wantonly destroys trees and slaughters
sleeping men on Christmas morning is just the type of guy this
country needs to get it going in the right direction.

WASHINGTON

(Beat.) You're not just saying that?

ELLIOT

No sir. I mean every word.

WASHINGTON

(Beat.) Merry Christmas, Elliot.

ELLIOT

Merry Christmas, General.

*(WASHINGTON turns forward again. Yankee Doodle plays solemnly.
Lights and SFX fade.)*

Explanation of the Secret

By watching thousands of improv scenes and observing actors and writers create shows, I have witnessed how both perceived, and actual, levels of status can affect an individual's ability to create freely. As a company, we have observed first-hand that if the levels of status can be flattened within a workgroup, it generally increases the comfort level, openness, and productivity of the group. By adhering to our belief that all ideas are equal, we must also view the creators of those ideas as equal. Taking it a step further, we also believe that everyone has the same creative potential, so it is easy for us to perceive all employees equally. We reinforce our theory of the status-free environment by aggressively involving several different experience levels of employees in the idea generation process.

Improvisational activity automatically lends itself to understanding the benefits of reducing status. By its very nature, improvisation demands that status be eliminated. For instance, if a member of an improv scene decides that he or she has more, or less, status than the others in the group, our scene has a fundamental problem. An individual who decides to increase his or her status will gain control of the scene and move it in a predetermined personal direction—that's not improvisation. Centering on self negatively affects the progress of the scene because very few actors can read minds. The team becomes paralyzed and is afraid to further the scene because they have no way of knowing, or understanding, what direction the "self-declared leader" has taken. Communication breaks down and confusion replaces creation for the remainder of the scene. The audience withdraws, sensing the scene has lost its natural progression and is no longer pure improvisation, unrehearsed, and spontaneous. This dynamic of "leader/follower" moves the improv scene from an organic flow of creativity to a structured and awkward "Simon says, stand on your toes and twirl."

A common improvisational jargon term is "follow the follower"—

meaning there is no leader and, at any given time, no *one* person is steering or dictating the direction of the scene. Within an improv scene, the organic flow of the scene determines the role of each actor. No one should ever feel obligated to lead the scene, but instead, should simply listen and follow the flow of the scene. Good improvisers understand and accept the role the scene requires and simply say yes to that role. If a group of improvisers performs ten successful scenes, each scene will naturally direct group members to take on different roles and contribute differently each time.

It is important not to confuse status with personal focus or commitment to a scene. At any given moment, one person may seem to be the focal point or center of the scene. This isn't necessarily a reflection of status; it may simply be the role the scene is asking that person to fulfill. There is a difference between an organic response to what the scene needs and manufactured status. Manufactured status is contrived, planned, or manipulated based on personal need for power, attention, or ego, and organic response is natural, free flowing, and recognizably spontaneous.

Identifying the Corporate Need

The negative implications of perceived status are clearest to me when I am working with a company that has a strong and dynamic leader. We won't name names here in order to protect the guilty and spare the innocent (or perhaps to spare the guilty and protect the innocent), but I am often in meetings with clients conducting a traditional brainstorming session to come up with new innovative solutions. Typically it is a relatively small conference room containing three to five company employees who have the same perceived status or rank. The information flows fluidly and the comfort level of the individuals is generally high. Then, the leader of the organization walks into the room. Suddenly, the energy in the room changes. Individuals who previously were speaking casually and freely are now selectively choosing their words and sneaking a peek at the team leader to measure his or her reaction to everything they say. The speed in which ideas are created comes to a grinding halt. Individual confidence in sharing points of view appears reduced. Why? Perhaps the leader who entered the room claims a longer title, a corner office, or a larger salary.

I don't want to give the impression that the only reason unhealthy status occurs is because of an oppressive or egotistical leader. Many times quite the opposite is true. I have worked with dozens of team leaders who genuinely want to empower their team and truly believe the ideas of their team members are equally innovative, and perhaps more creative, than their own. These leaders portray behavior of acceptance and encouragement and yet, for reasons beyond their control, their teams consistently decide to give them more status than they have asked for or even expected. The most successful brainstorming sessions make it difficult to identify the team leader because of the inherent sense of equality and no telltale signs of "status paralyzation."

Success Story: United Properties

United Properties Real Estate Company wanted to challenge its employees to improve the service they provided to one of their clients. After interviewing both the United Properties team that worked most closely with the client and key individuals from the client company, we discovered some communication obstacles. It was soon apparent these obstacles had been created because many of the United Properties employees were artificially giving the client more status than was appropriate for the working relationship.

The Brave New Workshop's goal was to help United Properties create an environment that enabled all points of view, opinions, and information to flow freely from both sides of the team. During a teambuilding workshop, we used improvisational exercises to demonstrate how reducing perceived status would lead to clearer communication and assist United Properties in providing the consultative expertise the client expected and needed. The result was a drastic increase in the volume of innovative ideas that the United Properties team produced for their client.

▲

"John Sweeney helped us work through a very difficult session with one of our major customers. He led us (laughing) through several exercises that emphasized the message of accepting all styles. As the participants quickly grew to trust him they extended that trust to each other and allowed us to begin a new and productive dialogue."

Jim Wadsworth, Director of Learning & Development,
United Properties LLC

The Secret of Creating a Statusless Environment is Working When

- Guests in a brainstorming session have difficulty identifying the group leader.
- Team members' style, communication, word choice, and diction remain consistent regardless of who's in the room.
- You no longer hear the term "we can discuss that issue offline," which usually means when the boss isn't here.
- It suddenly becomes okay to tease everyone about his or her golf score or haircut or dancing ability.
- Comments like "Yeah, if I was paid $100,000 a year, I'd have come up with a great idea too" disappear.
- The hoop that everyone previously needed to jump through has been retired and is on display in the company's hall of past behaviors.

The secret of Creating a Statusless Environment becomes most apparent in training sessions dealing with the subject of leadership.

BNW Product Application

The Brave New Workshop is regularly asked to help reduce the perceived status or inaccessibility of a management team or leader within a company or division. Many companies have come to realize that productivity, loyalty, and innovation increase when employees view their organizational leaders as true teammates. Conversely, if a leader is not considered a teammate, that leader's ability to positively affect the culture is diminished. Oftentimes, the leader is actually a hands-on person and has specific experience in the day-to-day operations of the company. Despite this reality, the team's perception is that the leader is somehow detached, and he or she is seen as an outsider. The reason for this perception is almost always due to a false sense of higher status. Time and time again clients call us in to help change this misperception of the leader.

An effective tool we use to counteract a false sense of status, either in the leader or as perceived by his or her team, is to have our actors perform sketches that portray real workplace scenarios. We write scripts appropriate to the challenges that the workforce is experiencing and feature the actual leader within the sketch, either literally in person or through an obvious portrayal by one of our actors. This often demonstrates to the team that the leader understands the issues they are facing and is approachable. It levels the playing field and reinforces the leader as an equal member of the team.

BNW Management Application

Like a good improv scene, the person who is in charge, or has the most responsibility for a project, is not necessarily the person who has the highest salary, most experience, or longest title at the Brave New Workshop. (Our theatre dog, Burt, is actually the one responsible for bestowing titles.) The process we use for selecting project managers is simple. We choose the person who is most passionate about the project and has a reasonable amount of skills and available time.

As improvisers, we understand that each scene may feature a different actor. This understanding also applies to our day-to-day business operations. It regularly shows itself in the form of a group of employees working together on several projects in which the leader of the group is different for each project. Additionally, "who's in charge" can and will change as priorities are shifted, old projects are completed, and new projects begin.

From Our Employees

I have been with the Brave New Workshop since the fall of 1986. During this time I have had the opportunity to sell tickets, hang Christmas lights, paint walls, prepare food, argue with telephone companies, replace roll towels in dispensers, take out garbage, clean toilets, move boxes, collect money, pay bills, and yes, I am even afforded the opportunity to take classes and write and perform. Why? Because I work in one of the greatest environments on the planet!

Our statusless environment occurs every day at the BNW. Each staff member is revered and respected for their individuality, ideas, and contributions. This genuine feel of comfort resounds in the walls and windowsills of the establishment. We all respond well to each other and "puzzle up." Rather than maintaining rigid corners or round edges we shape our individual pieces to fit the puzzle as it requires. As the company grows, it becomes more evident to me that this environment allows us to build upwards on a strong foundation.

At one point or another in the past eighteen years I have watched everyone do some job or task that could have in no way been a dictate of their job in an actual job description. Our working environment allows team members to explore and define tasks that they may never have been able to experience if they decided to hold onto the rigidity of what was "their" place. It allows people to move ahead into experiences that they can excel at. Julia provides an excellent example with her description of the tasks and challenges she has taken on. Again, why? Because no one told her that she was hired to be one thing and one thing only. There was no one to stop her from being what she truly wanted and needed to be. Everyone watched in awe and respect as she worked through this process.

The owners and leaders of the BNW have always set exceptional examples that have promoted this way of forward thinking. I have personally witnessed, first Dudley, now both John and Jenni, take on tasks that could have easily been written off as beneath their positions. I have seen them consistently roll up their shirtsleeves or "don a smock" to get the job done. It doesn't, of course, stop with them. Comfortable participation is relevant to any practical success story. How do you get people to participate? By consistently listening, learning, sharing, and letting them know and feel that their contribution is valuable and respected. This gives "the safety net" that holds up against rejection and isolation.

Our team is always willing to pitch in and provide assistance where and when needed. Tasks don't come to a halt because the "boss is coming." Mr. Haynes' story below is typical of all the staff's daily approach to tasks and projects at the BNW. Our statusless environment has created a dedicated group of staff members who are pleased to be working together and are able to accomplish great things.

Lynn Lanners, Director of Finance

One small example of a statusless environment was on a day that I entered the theatre in the morning after a party for a show opening. I knew that there was a show scheduled in the theatre that afternoon and that the theatre needed to be cleaned. The place was still a little bit of a mess from the night before. There were overflowing garbage cans, uneaten food, and a less than spotless stage.

Because of our statusless environment, I never hesitate to take care of things on my own. I didn't try to figure out whose job it was; I simply began to clean. As I was taking out the last of the garbage, a student arrived and asked, "You're the director of the school and you have to take out the garbage too?" I responded, "I don't have to; I get to." Of course, I received an interesting look from that student because he was used to a typical status-filled environment that assumed people in my position don't clean-up—that is someone else's job, and most, likely, that someone is lower on the organizational chart. At the Brave New Workshop, we don't have a lower or higher. We have people with various talents and abilities that all work together for the common goal of the theatre at all levels. I left that day feeling like I had contributed instead of becoming angry that someone else hadn't finished his or her work. Status or blame never entered my mind.

John Haynes, Director, Brave New Institute

SECRET 6

Create a Reward System that Recognizes Innovation & Creative Risk-Taking

BRAVE NEW WORKSHOP THEATRE

DATE: 01.19.01

SHOW: How to Try in Business Without Really Succeeding, or A Cubicle Named Desire

TITLE: "Successories"

DRAFT: FINAL

PREMISE:
Motivational posters that actually motivate

SETTING:
Art Department of the Successories company, very modern, all glass and chrome, perfectly designed by uncreative people to best facilitate creativity.

CHARACTERS:
SID: Extremely creative Successories poster artist, completely right-brained.

ALICE: SID's supervisor, thinks she is very creative, but she is not.

LION, ZEBRA, HANS, FRANC, WADING MAN: Vignette players

(Lights up on SID and ALICE at SID's workstation)

69

ALICE

There is no need to get defensive, SID. We're all a part of the Successories family, here. Remember, there is no "I" in team.

SID

You hate my ideas.

ALICE

We feel your ideas are very creative, SID, it's just . . .

SID

Just what?

ALICE

Our job here is to generate motivational material.

SID

Right.

ALICE

(She holds up a poster.) O.K., this is Emily's design for the Perseverance poster. See, it says "Perseverance: Only the strong shall prevail," and it has a beautiful sailboat on it. Very clean.

SID

O.K.

ALICE

(Holding up a poster.) O.K. This is your design for the same slogan. A picture of blood soaked lions devouring a zebra carcass. Now what, do you think, might be the problem with this?

SID

Nothing. You wanted an image that represented perseverance. It takes a pride of lions a long time to take down a zebra. Think about it.

(Lights up on a "lion" on the back of a "zebra" with her mouth clenched around the zebra's neck.)

LION

Dead yet?

ZEBRA

No.

LION

Dead yet?

ZEBRA

No.

LION

How 'bout now?

ZEBRA

Uh, nope.

LION

Damn.

(Cut back to office.)

SID

I felt this was the most powerful and honest
representation of the concept.

ALICE

Really?

SID

Yeah, and that sailboat picture doesn't make me want to
work harder, it just makes me have to pee.

ALICE

Fine! Why don't we talk about the line of new slogans
you have apparently taken upon yourself to create.

SID

You got my mock-ups?

ALICE

Oh yes. Here we have a poster reading, "Failure," with
a picture of the Hindenberg going down in flames.

SID

Yeah! I was thinking that the most effective motivator is
negative reinforcement. Remind people of what could
happen if they screw up! Remember?

(Cut to man standing, looking up.)

HANS

Oh look, the Hindenberg. *(Sounds of explosion.)*

HANS

Let's make sure this never happens
again. *(Cut back to office.)*

SID

And it never did.

ALICE

Oh . . . my. *(Angry now.)* Alright, SID, your last assignment
was "Teamwork." Simple. Just "Teamwork."
(She gets a second poster.) And here you have a picture of
a bunch of piranha devouring a human foot.

SID

There is no "I" in school.

ALICE

What?

SID

Isn't it obvious? One tiny piranha would take hours to
devour an entire man's foot, and clearly, the man would
get up and leave before it could finish. Imagine.

(Cut to tableau of man with feet dangling in water.)

MAN

Ouch. Ouch. Ouch. That's it, I've had it.

(Cut back to office.)

SID

However, an entire school of piranha could
easily succeed at the task.

(Cut to same man in the water screaming and thrashing around.)

MAN

Oh! They work together so efficiently!

(Cut back to office.)

SID

Teamwork at its finest.

ALICE

You are a strange, sick little man, SID, and you're fired!

SID

What are you trying to say?

ALICE

There is no "you" in here.

(Lights out.)

Explanation of the Secret

We've come to understand that, in general, people are more affected by their fear of creating the wrong idea than they are motivated by the excitement and passion of creating a truly innovative idea. Time and again I have observed our students, actors, and performers stifle and edit their own ideas, because of thoughts like, "everyone will think I'm foolish" or "what if it doesn't work." In order to counteract that habit, everyone at the BNW creates, and continually practices, a system that rewards people for taking risks and sharing their ideas.

> We've come to understand that, in general, people are more affected by their fear of creating the wrong idea than they are motivated by the excitement and passion of creating a truly innovative idea.

We have found that we need to reinforce and reward risk-taking and creative behavior at a 10 to 1 ratio in order to counter-balance human nature's fear of failure. In other words, we will praise someone ten times as much for producing a new idea, as we will critique him or her for a perceived "failure." We also realized that this high level of consistent 10 to 1 affirmation has to be in place for a long time before it will have a positive effect. Most of our students tell us that the most difficult thing to learn about improvisation is that there is no wrong answer or choice. Every day in class we watch educated and competent adults self-edit, bite their tongues, and deny their most instinctual and creative ideas because they believe that it is better to say or do nothing rather than to say or do the wrong thing.

As you may guess, this learned behavior to self-edit and judge takes a long time to unlearn. Most of our students learn it after about six months; however, some take longer, and some never do. Even with continuous positive reinforcement, the process can be frustrating, tedious, and require constant effort to overcome.

The simple system we use to reward risk-taking and innovative thinking is to shower the individual with affirmations and positive recognitions when they do take a risk or blurt out an unedited idea. We have also found the affirmations and recognitions that are most effective are oftentimes the simplest, most personal comments or actions. They do not necessarily have to be formal or public. It nearly goes without saying, but the sincerity in which you recognize these moments is essential. Patronizing language or tone, sarcastic or flippant comments will undermine that individual's ability to believe your affirmations and praise.

Remember that our goal is to improve the individual's skill to mass-produce ideas at the beginning of the idea generation process. By gradually increasing their idea generation, we help them become a more productive part of the team and ultimately improve the overall production and quality of our product and company.

Since we know that we need every idea at the outset to produce implementable ideas at the end, we recognize and reward contributions from the start with the same level of importance and recognition as we do on opening night.

Identifying the Corporate Need

I am reminded of the importance of our reward system for risk-taking and innovation when I emcee a company's annual awards events for their employees. I find myself thinking that the awards being given are exclusively for end results. It seems as if the only ideas that are recognized are the ones that have resulted in increased revenue, market share, or brand awareness. I listen to conversations of employees afterwards and am struck by how most of the discussion revolves around the result and not the steps needed to achieve the result. I find it hard to believe that the idea being recognized was conceived on its own and not somehow related or affected by hundreds of other ideas. Wouldn't it be fun to have an awards program after only 15 percent of the project was completed? Then, regardless of the outcome, individuals would be rewarded for their input, motivating them to increase their contributions by taking greater risks and thinking differently. Companies sometimes create awards for the most ideas or for the most outlandish ideas. This, at least, sends a message that it is okay to think differently and that employees will be recognized for all types of innovative contributions.

Success Story: Minnesota Timberwolves

The NBA's Minnesota Timberwolves basketball team was committed to creating an organization in which every employee was a spokesperson, a storyteller, and an ambassador for the team. To do this, they needed to create a new internal culture and help their employees change the way they perceived their jobs. They wanted everyone in the company—from their star player to their NBA Hall of Fame general manager to their receptionist—to view a part of their job as contributing and producing new and innovative ways to attract single ticket buyers, season ticket holders, luxury box customers, and corporate sponsors. They wanted to move away from the attitude of "that's not my job" and toward "wait, that's everyone's job."

To accomplish this, the Timberwolves initiated a financial incentive program designed to reward people within the organization for being part of an idea that brought in new sales. They also enlisted the Brave New Workshop to help senior management and employees look at risk-taking and innovation through the eyes of an improviser. Their employees responded favorably to the new incentive program and were inspired by the fact that everyone in the organization, including top management, was leading by example. It changed the way employees viewed their jobs and the way they viewed the entire organization. The Timberwolves successfully made the shift and motivated their employees to embrace the fact that their jobs included generating new ideas to make the customer experience better from start to finish.

▲

"I'm writing to tell you that your session with our management staff was fun, energetic, creative, inspirational,

motivating, and well worth the investment we made in your very unique approach to training . . . I will tell anyone who asks that if they are looking for a different experience, a change of pace, something that is unique, and that their staff will not forget, they should choose the Brave New Workshop. I know that you will absolutely 'deliver' for them."

Chris Wright, President, Minnesota Timberwolves

In one particular situation, the creative solution was that I would entertain the 19,000 fans of the Target Center as an overzealous, overweight, and eventually, shirtless fan. Part of the quirkiness of this idea was the fact that hopefully the audience would not know whether or not this ridiculous display of enthusiasm was set up or truly an inspired, jiggly team supporter. The idea worked better than anyone expected, and was featured on the local news, ESPN's "Sportscenter," and NBC's "Today Show." I am now affectionately known around the office as "Jiggly Boy." Here is a voicemail message I received from our client, the Minnesota Timberwolves, the day after our performance:

"Greatest thing I have EVER seen inside the arena. Unbelievable. You are . . . you're unbelievable. I must've got stopped 70 times last night in the concourse from either outrage that we'd take out a guy havin' fun in the stands to, 'Alright, is that really real? Did you guys set this up?' Greatest thing I have ever seen. Unbelievable. In fact, last night in the first quarter I was sitting with my counterpart from the Mavericks, and I told him, I said , 'Hey, watch this.' Here's the way I set it up, I said, 'Watch this guy who sits over in Section 128, he's one of our Superfans, he's just tons of fun. The first time, he goes, 'This guy's hilarious!' Then the second time, he was literally on the ground laughing. And then the guys came and escorted you out, he was like, 'What's goin' on? What's happenin'? Why are you doin' this.' So I kind of tipped him off as to what was goin' on. Funniest thing I've ever seen. Absolutely classic."

Jeff Munneke, Vice President of Fan Relations and Guest Services
Minnesota Timberwolves

The Secret of Creating a Reward System for Innovation and Risk-Taking is Working When

- People have more conversations recalling the steps taken to create a proposal rather than the highlights of "the pitch."
- Individuals display notebooks full of concepts and ideas prominently in their office instead of plaques recognizing the end product or replications of whatever was ultimately delivered to market.
- Individuals begin to keep track of gross idea generation figures as well as the outcome of successful idea implementation.
- You develop your own necessary ratio for how many ideas you need to generate to find the one idea that is implementable. Is it 50 to 1 or 100 to 1 or 30 to 1?
- Some team members acquire a sense of bravado regarding their reputation as a "high producer" of bulk ideas at the *beginning* of the idea generation process.

The secret of Creating a Reward System That Recognizes Innovation and Risk-Taking is best suited to training sessions that focus on leadership.

BNW Product Application

The clearest example of how we use a reward system that recognizes risk-taking and idea innovation comes, once again, in our process of creating our shows. The only time we monitor, track, and recognize an individual's success or level of contribution is during the initial stages, or at the beginning, of the idea generation process.

In a usually non-competitive, egalitarian environment our sense of healthy competition shows itself only during this phase of the funnel process. The individual team members and director are very much aware of how many of the six hundred Master Inspiration List ideas are produced by each team member. *(See chapter 10, Our Creative Funnel Process.)*

In the next step of our process, we complete the Key Elements— the basic components—of the ideas selected. It is the only time we document and actually assign an individual's name to an idea. The director distributes a progress sheet each morning that clearly identifies which team members have produced which Key Elements. If one individual has completed fifteen and another has only completed two, the difference will be openly discussed. The director clearly recognizes, and rewards, individuals for the volume of ideas they create and the amount of work they provided in the beginning stage of idea generation.

Conversely, at the end of our process, during preview week, opening night, and throughout the run of the show, people are *not* recognized for their individual contribution to the completed and final sketches. In most cases, no one can even recall who actually came up with the original idea for the sketch or song. In short, we encourage, recognize, and reward our team members for contributing volumes of ideas at the beginning of our process and are purposely unaware of who should be recognized at the end of the process. The completed product we present to our customers truly becomes a team success as a result of collaboration.

BNW Management Application

Everything we do at the Brave New Workshop is about rewarding people for taking risks and thinking differently. It is such a regular mode of operation that it seems to be more of a description of our culture rather than a policy or human resource initiative. Many times it is as if we have reversed the typical system in the sense that people seem to be fearful of *not* taking risks or *not* thinking innovatively. We actually have to remind ourselves that sometimes it is okay to simply come up with an idea that is logical or predictable. In a culture that has risk-taking as its norm, we observe a healthy sense of competition in who takes the biggest risk and is the current "champion of innovation."

One of the most common phrases heard in improvisational training is that "you must make everyone on stage look better than yourself." That sense of camaraderie and esprit de corps is clearly evident in the daily recognition witnessed throughout our offices. I often observe our employees spending much more time congratulating and recognizing the risk-taking and innovation of fellow employees than trying to sing their own praises or manipulate recognition for their own successes.

We spend our days encouraging each other to be more of ourselves and to trust our own organic sense of what is innovative. We believe that if we are successful at accomplishing that, the results will automatically follow. And, as oversimplified as it may sound, we try to maintain an environment in which people think, "every time I come up with a new idea it feels good, and every idea I produce is met with respect and initial acceptance."

From Our Employees

I'm not exactly a risk-taker. In fact, I couldn't be more paralyzed with pleasing people if I were a politician, and I couldn't be more aware of the importance of maintaining balance if I were a tightrope walker. And yet, I find my-self in a work environment that challenges both of these tendencies, and I love it. When I first started at the BNW, I had miniscule theatre experience and was extremely hesitant to share my point of view for fear that it was sub-standard or just downright ignorant. I was intimidated by the quick wit and keen insight that my co-workers seemed to display daily. It was worst during staff meetings when I continually found myself thinking "how did you ever man-age that?" or "don't you have to write that down?" When it came to my turn, my head would spin, and I'd completely lose track of what I wanted to say. And yet, every time I did manage to spout out an idea or project update, it was met with enthusiastic response. From day one, my co-workers acceptance and support never wavered. Of course, not every idea was executed because some were absolute crap, but my teammates always supported the fact that I had shared it with them. Zippity forward three years and my biggest challenge is to stop talking and take action. I so enjoy the idea generation process and sharing ideas that I literally have to force myself into the next step to avoid getting bogged down in all the wonderful possibilities. Now, if you can imagine, I look forward to staff meetings. Each week, amazing people share amazing visions, and all I can think of is, "I'm helping to make this happen." That and, "Oh, and by the way, freaks, I've got a really bad idea I'd love to share . . ."—the worst are applauded and the best are improved.

Dawn Hopkins, Director of Corporate Services Marketing
and Internet Technology

SECRET 7

Yes, First!

BRAVE NEW WORKSHOP THEATRE

DATE: 01.19.01

SHOW: How to Try in Business Without Really Succeeding, or A Cubicle Named Desire

TITLE: "Vinyl Siders"

DRAFT: FINAL

PREMISE:
What would happen if a telemarketer was met with a willing customer?

SETTING:
A telemarketing office and a suburban kitchen.

CHARACTERS:
DANIELLE: College student majoring in English who is working as a telemarketer for extra cash.

BOSWELL HENKINS: A very approachable, father figure type of guy. You'd trust your only child with him. Piano teacher.

BILL ZELINSKI: Wendy's cook who has watched too many old movies.

(Lights up on BILL ZELINSKI on the phone flipping burgers at Wendy's.)

83

BILL

I'll tell you something, missy. You are the paragon of all
that is evil and wrong on this earth. I hope you die slowly
in the belly of a python.

(Cross to DANIELLE with headset in front of computer.)

DANIELLE

The belly of a python! Well, at least you were original, freak.

(She types, phone rings, BOSWELL enters his living room, picks up phone.)

BOSWELL

Hello?

DANIELLE

Yes, is Mr. Boswell Henkins available?

BOSWELL

I'm him! I'm Boswell Henkins! I was just about ready to
sit down to dinner, but what can I do for you?

DANIELLE

How are you this evening, sir?

BOSWELL

I don't think it's possible for me to be better!

DANIELLE

Good! I'm calling from VinylGuard, the most durable
maintenance-free vinyl siding available. This durable siding
won't rot, peel, chip, flake, or blister. We believe your home is
your castle. I have quite a deal for you, sir.

BOSWELL

Go on, please! I must know!

DANIELLE

Do you worry about the resale value of your home? Have you
ever had termites or wood boring insects? Have you wasted
precious hours painting and repainting your home—

BOSWELL

Yes! The answer to all of your questions is yes!

DANIELLE

O-Okay. Then VinylGuard is the solution for you.

BOSWELL

Sold! Sign me up!

DANIELLE

I'm sorry?

BOSWELL

I said sign me up. Your persuasive sales pitch
has left me positively reeling.

DANIELLE

What?

BOSWELL

My "castle" is currently imprisoned in a terribly old, hand carved
marble. Your vinyl siding sounds young and daring.

DANIELLE

So you actually want vinyl siding?

BOSWELL

Yes indeed-ee!

DANIELLE

Okay then Mr. Boswell Henkins! Please be informed that
any and all terms of this deal are irrevocable.

BOSWELL

Sounds perfect!

DANIELLE

That means you can't back out.

BOSWELL

Who would want to? It just keeps getting better!

DANIELLE

The only colors it comes in are raisin and off-raisin.

BOSWELL

Sounds delicious.

DANIELLE

Mr. Boswell Henkins, you should be informed that our vinyl siding has been proven to cause excessive hair growth and impotence in laboratory rats.

BOSWELL

I'm balding and celibate!

DANIELLE

I can't let you do this! This is crazy sir! This is a crappy product! I do deserve to die in the belly of a python!

BOSWELL

Your blunt honesty has led me to ask if you sell storm doors!

(Black out.)

Explanation of the Secret

Saying yes to new ideas is by far the most widely understood concept and most basic skill that improvisers use. Building an improvisational scene is an accumulative and reactive exchange. The first improviser declares a point of view or idea. The second improviser says yes to the idea and then adds to it. This is universally referred to in the improvisation community as the concept of "yes, and," but we refer to it as, "yes, first." The opposite of this concept would be "no, but."

As we mentioned in chapter 1 *(Accepting All Ideas)*, the improvisational scene requires improvisers to figure out who they are, where they are, what needs to get done, who will do it, accomplish what they have set out to do, and resolve the scene in a matter of two to three minutes—while being funny in front of a live audience. Because of this hyperspeed environment in which improv is produced and performed, saying no to an idea at the beginning of a scene, will lead to a temporary shutdown and require a new set of declarations to restart the action. Improvisers simply don't have the luxury of time to say no.

At the Brave New Workshop, we believe the true value of saying yes to an idea and then adding to that idea is propulsion, like Jiffy-pop popcorn. *(See chapter 10, Our Creative Funnel Process, step 1: Idea Generation.)* Because our goal is to rapidly produce hundreds of ideas, it is vital and necessary to say yes to fill our funnel with ideas at the very beginning. We find that truly innovative solutions are rarely conceived in their executable form at infancy. By saying yes to those ideas first, they are propelled through our funnel process and towards the innovative end result.

Remember, we are talking about the *first 15 percent* of the idea generation process. We are simply saying yes to the potential that exists within the idea. When we say "yes, first," we are not saying we should approve a budget,

> *When we say "yes, first," we are not saying we should approve a budget, staffing, or that the idea will be automatically implemented.*

staffing, or that the idea will be automatically implemented. We are simply saying yes to the idea in order to allow it to reach its full potential. Once we say yes to an idea, it begins to take on the characteristic of fuel for idea generation.

We are certainly aware that saying yes to every idea is drastically different than typical behavior. Many people in our improvisation classes initially find it difficult to follow the rules of a simple class-room exercise in which they literally must say the word "yes" before beginning their next sentence of dialogue. This is equally difficult for participants in our corporate training workshops. Ironically, we are often asked, "What is the single most important skill I need in order to become a better improviser or to produce more innovative solutions in my workplace?" The answer is, "Say yes, first."

Often, we are confronted with the exclamation, "but what if I disagree with the person's idea?" "So what?" we commonly reply. There is a huge difference between agreeing to implement an idea and simply acknowledging the intrinsic value and potential an idea possesses. Once an individual is practiced in the skill of saying yes, they can retain their own point of view while simultaneously supporting their teammates point of view, even if they disagree.

We encourage everyone in our organization to self monitor and maintain a record of the number of times they say "yes, first" as well as "no, but." We challenge you to do the same. If you can increase the number of times your response to others' ideas is yes, you are undoubtedly increasing the innovative potential of both you and your teammates.

Identifying the Corporate Need

I am most impacted by the concept of "yes, first" when I force my-self to remember how it was for me as a young associate working in the pressure-filled industry of corporate real estate. I remember too many instances in which I would approach one of my superiors with a new, and perhaps even innovative, idea. Their response often made me wonder if I had accidentally asked them, "Could you please tell me what's wrong with this really stupid idea?" At that moment, I felt their main goal was to stop the consideration of the idea before discussion even started. They immediately took on the role of critic, not partner. Often, they spent more time dissecting and explaining what was wrong with the idea than I spent creating it. So what could I have done differently? Perhaps I presented the idea in a way that sought approval and not collaboration? Maybe my approach cried, "critique me, critique me." The truth is what I really wanted from them was to help me expand and improve the idea. Oftentimes, this type of interaction created a feeling of rivalry and competition instead of teamwork and collaboration. Now, with the insight I've gained as an improviser, I realize that if we had both approached the idea with the principle of "yes, first," we may have been able to move forward together to create a truly unique result.

I wonder how many innovative, and perhaps miraculous, ideas never got a chance to see the light of day, let alone come to fruition. What a different world this would be if the individuals who created those ideas had first shared them with someone who understood the value of "yes, first."

NBA Entertainment

We were so successful in our work with the Minnesota Timber-wolves professional basketball team we received an invitation to work with all of the teams in the league. Specifically, the National Basketball Association asked us to train and help facilitate a brainstorming session at the 2004 NBA Game Presentation Workshop held at NBA Entertainment Studios in New Jersey. Game Presentation staff members from each of the NBA's thirty franchises attended. The stated goal of the workshop was to foster a creative dialogue among all the teams and share existing and new best practices throughout the league.

The three-hour morning session introduced the 8 Secrets contained in this book. A series of participatory improvisational exercises were then used to reinforce the secrets. The level of excitement and energy continued to build throughout the morning and dozens of volunteers willingly participated in each new exercise. The secret of "yes, first!" was emphasized throughout the training session. This group had significant experience in their individual roles within their organizations and the perception "they had tried everything" had become an obstacle for them. There seemed to be a tendency to dwell more on why new ideas *couldn't* work rather than saying "yes" to why new ideas *could* work. In addition, like many of us, this group had already executed dozens of successful ideas over a considerable number of years and had a case of "idea drought."

The training session was successful in creating an environment of enthusiastic collaboration and risk-free idea sharing. After lunch, a handful of teams gave presentations on best practices that had been successful in their franchise. The Brave New Workshop facilitated the dialogue following each presentation. The pace and excitement of the question and answer period was anything but typical. The amount of valuable information shared between the people in the room was staggering.

The remainder of the day was spent in a brainstorming session. The group was formally introduced to the Brave New Workshop Funnel Process *(see chapter 10)*. After a few more improvisational exercises to get back in the mode of "yes, first," an initial idea list was created. In a matter of minutes, one hundred topics were generated as possible brainstorming candidates. The group then quickly and efficiently selected the three most important and urgent topics for the upcoming season. These topics included ideas for: (1) "theme nights" to attract specific segments of the community, (2) timeout activities to include children, and (3) improving the game experience for audience members seated in the upper bowl of arenas.

In a matter of hours, the group, who did not work together on a daily basis and in some ways may be considered competitors, generated more than 1,000 ideas for the selected topics—many of which you may have witnessed in your hometown NBA arena.

This session clearly validated the "yes, first!" equation of attitude plus energy plus innovation equals productivity.

▲

"It was a pleasure working with you and your team. The output of ideas from the brainstorming session was phenomenal and we look forward to the teams implementing some of them in the upcoming season. I'd be happy to serve as a reference for any future clients as our experience with you could not have been more positive."

Greg Lehmann, Director
National Basketball Association Entertainment

The Secret of "Yes, First!" is Working When

- Your brainstorming meetings begin to take on "explosive" characteristics as the "yes, first" affect multiplies and heightens ideas.

- You find that an increase in the number of ideas being fed through your own version of the creative process results in higher levels of innovative productivity.

- You begin to notice and react to your own "no, but" responses and the "no, but" responses of others.

- You notice a drastic reduction in how many times a brainstorming session gets bogged down by discussions of all the reasons why an idea can't work.

- You begin to hear "no, but" fewer times than at a J-Lo photo session.

The secret of "Yes, First!" is a particularly strong component of training sessions that deal with the subjects of innovation and change management.

BNW Product Application

Summer is a horrible time to own a theatre in the state of Minnesota. On Friday afternoons the two major highways leading north out of Minneapolis and St. Paul become a virtual parking lot as the traditional migration to the cabin "up North" occurs. And, if you can believe it, Minnesotan's love their cabins even more than they love live comedy. As a way to find an alternative source of income for the summer months, someone at the BNW came up with the idea to market our touring capabilities to the northern Minnesota lodges and resorts.

When this idea was presented to the person responsible for marketing and selling this aspect of our business, she had her reservations. She had dealt with resorts before and didn't think there was a huge opportunity. She is an improviser, however, and simply said "yes, first!"

She began calling the lodges most likely to be interested by our proposal and was immediately presented with information that supported what she had presumed—they weren't interested. Then, the power of "yes, first" became clear. By moving forward with the idea and taking action, she found out that several of the lodges had relationships with the local civic centers or community theatres. The resorts often sent their guests to see the local productions and touring shows these venues booked throughout the summer. That information had never come up in our brainstorming sessions when we discussed ways to create additional summer income. Most likely, we wouldn't have discovered that opportunity without her decision to say, "yes, first," instead of, "no, but."

We were able to approach these venues and book performances with them for the first time in our company's history. As a result, the out-state touring program is a great contributor to our revenues during the months of July and August.

BNW Management Application

We recently began using a new format for our weekly staff meetings. It is a drastic departure from the old format, which was pretty typical. Previously, each staff member had a place on the agenda and would give an update on the status of projects within his or her area of responsibility. Many times this information was repetitive, especially for those who were part of the project team and already knew what was going on. Several of our employees declared that they thought revamping the format of our staff meetings would lead to a better use of our time together and would produce greater opportunity for individual insights and talents to be shared with each other. Doing so meant we had to rely much more heavily on our Intranet to exchange general information and keep abreast of current projects. Instead of saying "no, but," we upgraded the features of our Intranet to include calendar scheduling, open discussion boards, and stronger security. One "yes, first" for a good idea led to another "yes, first" for advancing our technology. Our staff meetings are now used as a forum to generate new ideas and share best practices at the beginning stages of project management.

Each week, after each of the BNW staff have shared with the group a thirty-second "success story," we quickly move on to the predetermined brainstorming topic of the week. The topic is typically a project that one of the staff members is struggling to get off the ground. As always, the goal of the session is to look at the situation differently and use the idea generation model to provide the staff member in need with volumes of new insights, ideas, and possible solutions. No one in the room critiques or analyzes what is wrong with the current situation; we simply spend all of our time producing new ideas as a gift to the staff member whose situation we are brainstorming.

From Our Employees

Examples of "yes, first" at work are all over the place here. We often wind up solving a problem differently than we planned—but arriving at a better solution than we would have otherwise.

When I first started working here and heard people talking about the improvisational term "yes, and," I thought it referred only to dealing with other individuals on stage. Now, I realize you can "yes, and" situations. You can "yes, and" your car; you can "yes, and" the weather. I do it all the time, or at least I'm aware of it, and it's certainly not because I have a great deal of improv in my background. (I'm a total "civilian" when it comes to improv training and experience, certainly when compared to the rest of the team!)

I find that as I'm working on a problem, if I get a negative result or a circumstance I didn't expect but I keep saying "yes"—those results just redirect me rather than shutting me down. It makes failure impossible. Being in sales, this has become invaluable to me.

Erin Farmer, Director of Group Sales

I think a strong example of how saying "yes" impacts our process is the final script of the show "Total Recall 2: The Governator." This show was something of a departure from other shows we have done in that it looked more like a single storyline than a series of sketches. However, this was not the original intention when we began the writing process. The show started out to be a collection of loosely related sketches. The writers composed these sketches with no real intention of them fitting together.

Somewhere along the line, the idea was presented that maybe all the sketches could become part of a central storyline or plot about the California recall election. There would be a central plot and sketches would be modified, cut, or newly written in order to make this plot line work. Essentially, the idea meant re-imagining all the work that had been done up to that point. Many groups would have said "no" to this idea for convenience if nothing else. However, the cast responded by saying yes, and work began.

Not only did the cast have to say yes to the process of putting the show together in a new way, they also had to say yes to the work they had already done. Sketches that seemingly had nothing to do with the plot were given an equal chance of making the final cut alongside sketches that were directly related. As a result of this open mindset, a number of sketches were creatively included in the story-line and went on to become big hits. The show was a huge success, and all because the group said yes to a new idea of how to do things.

Caleb McEwen, Artistic Director, Actor, Writer

SECRET 8

Perceiving Change as Fuel

BRAVE NEW WORKSHOP THEATRE

DATE: 01.18.01

SHOW: How to Try in Business Without Really Succeeding, or A Cubicle Named Desire

TITLE: "Merger Mania!"

DRAFT: FINAL

PREMISE:

A customer goes into a bank to deposit a check and is subject to an amazing amount of corporate takeovers.

MERGER: n: 1. a statutory combination of two or more corporations by the transfer of the properties to one surviving corporation.

SETTING:

Help desk at Norwest Bank. Cherry wood waiting tables, evergreen and plum carpet.

CHARACTERS:

TELLER: Eager, competent, and full of energy. Wears headset.

CUSTOMER 1: Bright, urban professional. Tired after a long day at work.

CUSTOMER 2: Provides ending.

(Lights up on TELLER with headset on talking to her boss: "Thanks Bill; I'll check out" etc.)

TELLER

Welcome to Norwest! How may I help you?

CUSTOMER I

Yes, I have some deposits to make and a cash withdrawal.

TELLER

Here you go! Here at Wells Fargo, formerly Norwest,
we're happy—

CUSTOMER I

(Holding deposit slip.) Wells Fargo? Oh, yeah, right. *(Looks around.)*
Wells Fargo. But this is still Norwest, though, right?

TELLER

Yes, Wells Far—Whoops! No . . . Actually, we have just been
bought out by People's Bank. *(Changes sign on desk.)*

CUSTOMER I

P-People's . . . ? I'm with Norwest. *(Quickly.)* Wells Fargo Norwest.

TELLER

Ahhhh . . . A-A-A-And this is your lucky day! *(Changes sign again.)*
We are, once again, Norwest. I mean, Wells Fargo . . . Norwest . . .
(Correcting self.) Wells Fargo.

CUSTOMER I

(Staring at TELLER uneasily.) Okay. *(Looks down.)* I'd like to
deposit this into my savings . . .

TELLER

(Hiding face.) Welcome to U.S. West! Now Qwest! For what city?

CUSTOMER I

(Looking around.) What? *(Pause.)*
I mean . . . what?

TELLER

What city? *(Pointing adamantly to phone.)* Pick up the phone!

CUSTOMER I

(Into receiver, frightened.) Hello. I'd like to make a deposit.

TELLER

Please hold. Your call is important to us and will be answered in the order that it was received.

(CUSTOMER I stares at TELLER in silence)

CUSTOMER I

(While waiting on the phone.) Hi.

TELLER

Hi. *(Pause.)*

CUSTOMER I

Okay, stop that! *(Slams phone down.)* Just forget it! I'm leaving! If you can't help me I'll find someone who can!

TELLER

Yes! Yes I can! *(Picks up sign on ground.)* Welcome to Wells Fargo!

CUSTOMER I

Yeah, and I'm suppose to believe—

TELLER

(Hysterical.) Shut it! Please! Give me the check! I am Wells Fargo! I am Wells Fargo!

CUSTOMER I

Okay! I'd like twenty bucks back in cash!

TELLER

(Thrusting check back to CUSTOMER I and knocking sign off desk.)
Sorry! I can't do that!

CUSTOMER I

Why?!

TELLER

Because I'm a sandwich artist! Welcome to Wells Fargo Subway
brought to you by Microsoft!

CUSTOMER I

(Screaming.) I don't want a sandwich!

TELLER

(Hysterical.) I know! But we have signature sauce!

(Pause as TELLER gets another message.)

CUSTOMER I

Who are you?

TELLER

Thank you for visiting iwhack.com.
We provide Internet solutions.

CUSTOMER I

What does that mean?

TELLER

I have absolutely no idea! *(Excitedly.)* But our company has a
market capitalization of 2.4 billion dollars!
(Screams, which causes CUSTOMER I to scream.)
I'm rich!

CUSTOMER I

Congratulations!

TELLER

Whoa! Ease up! We're bankrupt!
We groom pets now!

CUSTOMER I

(Desperate.) My cousin has a dog!

TELLER

That's nice, but we've just been bought by AOL. You've got mail!

CUSTOMER I

Really? Can I read it?

TELLER

(Making busy signal sound.) No! We're busy! Try again later!

CUSTOMER I

Listen—

TELLER

Buenos Dias! Bee-en Ven—ee-dos de Banco Bil Bano Vis Sky Ano!

CUSTOMER I

Banco! You're a banco?

TELLER

Nein! Welkolmen! Deutsche Telekom!

CUSTOMER I

Listen! I want Norwest! Not Deutsche-Pets-Fargo-whatever—

TELLER

(Putting sign on desk.) No need!
Welcome to American Express!

CUSTOMER I

Okay, wait a minute!
I work for American Express.

TELLER

So you're here to take my shift! Great!
(Hands headset to CUSTOMER 1.)

(CUSTOMER 2 enters. CUSTOMER 1 stands there dumbfounded with headset in hand.)

CUSTOMER 1

Welcome to American Express! No—wait—we've just been bought out by Marshall Fields.

CUSTOMER 2

Hey, I remember when this place used to be a Daytons!

(Blackout or transition.)

Explanation of the Secret

Improvisers view change quite differently than most people. We often hear that many people are adverse to change and find comfort in stability and consistency. Unfortunately, for the improviser, if a scene is not changing, then it is stagnant, repetitive, and predictable—and our customers go away.

It is from this point of view that we approach our perception and appreciation for change. We do not see change as an interruption of what is reliable and consis-

> *We do not see change as an interruption of what is reliable and consistent, but as an exciting exploration toward what is next.*

tent, but as an exciting exploration toward what is next. Change is not a necessary evil, but rather a vehicle of opportunity that allows us to discover and heighten the next part of the scene.

Our need for change is so strong that we are constantly trying to create new skills that will allow us to promote and ignite change. We are not unhappy with the current situation. Instead, we have come to understand that our most innovative ideas come by traveling through a process driven by action and focused on forward movement. The fuel we use to create this forward motion is change.

Another contrast we found in our relationship with change compared to many of the companies we encounter is that we have no need to predict or forecast the end result. We do not worry about how impending change might affect us. This freedom from the need to predict or worry about the future allows us to focus all of our energy on the current situation. As improvisers we use the term "being in the moment." Mathematically, this is a wonderful device as it allows all of our focus, attention, and energy to be given to the current task without diluting that energy worrying about future variables. We're confident we have the skills to deal with whatever situation comes next, and we genuinely look forward to the new reality that lies just beyond the next episode of change.

Identifying the Corporate Need

It is my observation that one of the biggest shifts in the American workplace in recent years is the perception of change. After the collapse of Enron, the depressed economy, and hundreds of other unexpected, almost unbelievable changes in our world, I don't think many people still feel that a long-term, consistent, non-changing workplace is the norm or, for that matter, even possible. The ability to deal with constant change is almost a required skill for corporate employment.

Though people may still have the tendency to crave stability, the positive effect of this new perception is that companies no longer look at *change management skills* as solely a way to gain advantage over the competition or as a philosophical soft skill. Increasingly, businesses are learning to find opportunity within change and consequently are training their employees to do the same. Most companies now view change as inevitable and include it as a core element in their long-term strategic business plan. Industries that historically considered change a deterrent to profitability now embrace it as an opportunity. Companies that built a reputation as unwavering in their approach to business have now found new insights in their approach to change.

I believe there are some wonderful benefits in this new understanding of change in corporate America. The skills that companies have developed as a way to deal with change are also producing new and surprising secondary benefits, including a less rigid approach to how they see their business and a blossoming sense of innovation as a key requirement to success in the marketplace.

Success Story: Infinity Broadcasting/WCCO Radio

Like many sales organizations, the sales force of WCCO radio needed to re-examine how they approached selling their products. The market had changed, the competition had increased, and customers were constantly demanding more for less. It was clear that members of the sales team were going to have to adapt the sell. This seemed especially hard for the senior sales reps who had sold ad spots the same way for many years.

The fundamental difference in the way they needed to approach their business was that customers and prospects no longer just expected a simple rate sheet and description of the time and duration of the ad spots. They expected a marketing package that incorporated several programs and products and dispersed their marketing message through a number of media. This "package approach" included the incorporation of other media buys, the forming of relationships with other marketing partners, and the creation of media events or initiatives. This was a much broader and subjective approach than simply selling the customer twenty 30-second radio ads at a certain rate per ad.

The management of WCCO radio had incredible foresight in seeing this change ahead of the competition and proactively decided to retool the skill set of their sales force. First, the sales force was armed with a new set of products and promotions that would allow them to offer their customers what they needed. WCCO radio hired the Brave New Workshop to show their sales force how to approach the sales process as an improvisational scene. We were able to expose the group to the principles of perceiving change as fuel and help them say "yes, first!" to the new opportunity. The sales force responded positively both to the new types of products they could offer and to the new way they approached selling radio advertising. The ultimate result was a drastic recapturing of market share and a record sales year.

▲

"Stepping into the world of improvisation as a training tool was a new experience for WCCO radio. The results were quite impressive. Using Brave New Workshop for our opening training session on creativity and change management not only addressed those topics in a

most informative and entertaining manner, but set the tone for our entire meeting. The response from our sales staff was very positive. We now have alternatives to PowerPoint, videos, lectures, and other mundane training methods. The staff engaged in training both physically and mentally. Creativity in sales is a difficult subject to address. You made it come alive and broke new ground for many of our account executives.

"Thank you for helping us move our sales effort to the next level. I would be happy to recommend your Improvisation Training to other Infinity Radio Stations."

Dick Carlson, Vice President of Sales WCCO Radio

The Secret of Perceiving Change as Fuel is Working When

- Change is not viewed as an obstacle to idea generation, but rather embraced with excitement of things to come.

- Less time is spent worrying about "what ifs" and "what mights" and more time is spent responding appropriately to current necessary changes.

- Employees are able to create consistently, regardless of what changes are happening around them. Change will no longer signal a decrease in productivity or an increase in fear.

- Employees begin working toward creating change because they understand it is a propellant needed to find the next bit of innovation.

The secret of Perceiving Change as Fuel is clearly apparent in training sessions that deal with the subjects of change management and innovation.

BNW Product Application

Simple and almost mundane changes can produce expansive and innovative outcomes. In writing sketches for our shows, we approach each scene through an examination of its most basic components or Key Elements. *(See chapter 10, Our Creative Funnel Process, Step 2: Refinement.)* If, at any point within the creation process, we are stuck or feel the script simply isn't as good as it could be, we may alter one of the Key Elements to drastically change the scene. For instance, we might choose to change the environment in which the scene takes place, one of the major plot points or characters, or even something as simple as a costume. The following is an example of how a single change can have wonderful impact on the entire product. The sketch was a simple two-person scene in which two men were having a heated debate over the issues of capital punishment in a diner. One man was passionate in his views in support of capital punishment, while the other was equally passionate in his opposition to the issue. By simply changing the location of the scene from a diner to the execution chamber of a federal penitentiary with one man in the chair and the other man about to pull the switch, the script went from "okay" to "riveting." The dialogue, characters, and everything else in the scene remained the same. Yet that simple change increased the tension, energy, and excitement of the scene tenfold.

BNW Management Application

Like many companies, we often struggle with changes that will somehow alter tried and true traditions. There are many things we have done at the theatre year after year for more than forty-five years. These operational traditions almost seem to have a personality of their own. They are somehow insulated from change, and we tend to treat them as a sacred cow because of their history. Theatre can be an odd business that way. There is a sense of superstition involved in these sacred traditions.

The following example demonstrates that the Brave New Workshop is not entirely immune to this heightened sense of change adversity. For as long as anyone can remember, the BNW performed two shows on Friday night, one at 7:30 P.M. and another one at 10 P.M. and two shows on Saturday night, again at 7:30 P.M. and 10 P.M. However, a 2003 review of our attendance figures clearly showed that, although attendance was holding steady, our Friday night shows were less popular than in years gone by. A suggestion was made to perform only one show on Friday nights at 8 P.M. At first, I was incredibly adverse to that recommendation. A "two-show Friday night" was so entrenched in the way we did business, and in my perceived understanding of customer expectations, that I fought it tooth and nail. I remember thinking that if I decided to eliminate one of the Friday night performances, hundreds of alumni would call, cursing me for changing this fundamental operational tradition. But the calls never came and, since we have made the change, our total Friday night attendance has increased by nearly 20 percent. In fact, the end result was that even though we reduced the number of shows we offered, we increased the total number of customers who attended. Go figure.

From Our Employees

John and I were so excited in 1998 to relocate our theatre and offices to the swanky, clean, new space in the Calhoun Square retail complex, just a few blocks from the dusty, historic building we had inhabited since 1965. It was our dream to bring this historic theatre "to the next level."
At the time we thought "the next level" meant more seats for our customers in a less cramped theatre, professionally installed lights and sound, parking for our patrons in an attached ramp, offices with matching carpet, and two NEW restrooms, one for the gals and one for the guys! So we moved the whole dang operation down the road to Cal-

houn Square, and we took with us forty years of history, a dozen staff, a few hammers, and dreams of a bigger, better theatre and lots of profits. Long story short, our dream did not go as we had hoped. Yes, we enjoyed pretty offices with windows overlooking the corner of hip and hip. And yes, we enjoyed shiny, clean restrooms where patrons could actually gather and strike up conversations. And yes, we enjoyed an abundance of steady air conditioning in the summer and ample heat in the winter. But not everything worked out as we had planned. Although our revenues increased, they did not increase at a level that would cover the drastic increase in operational expenses associated with our new space. We could no longer risk the future of our 40-year-old history in exchange for the fancy digs.

Three years after we moved in, we made the risky decision to go back to our historic, dusty, hole in the wall theatre and end our lease in Calhoun Square. We felt it was necessary to keep the theatre going and we decided we'd do anything to keep the doors open, even if it meant admitting our mistakes and going back to a smaller space. It's difficult to admit something did not go the way you had planned, and even more difficult to ask your staff and employees to follow your lead once again. Just three years earlier we had asked our staff to trust us, put in the extra work, roll up their sleeves, and follow us into this new venture. Now, three years later, we were asking them to not only role up their sleeves again, but to also give up their fancy offices, parking passes, and private desks.

We were worried that a few might jump ship. We were worried that the staff would sigh and say "what now?" But being blessed with incredible employees who truly do live improvisationally, their response was nothing but positive. Not only did they see the change as necessary, but also the impending move seemed to fuel their creative juices.

Rather than dwelling on our failures, the staff immediately embraced the change and jumped in asking "how can we make this work to our benefit?"

They said "yes, first" to our declaration of the need to do something drastic, and then moved ahead aggressively in making our new situation successful. Our creative director and cast of actors said "yes, first" by deciding to make the move back to the old space the theme of the next show. Our marketing staff said "yes, first" by capitalizing on the move back to the old space by getting our founder, Dudley Riggs, involved and pitching stories about the "Brave New Workshop going home." And our front of house staff enlisted dozens of volunteers and students in giving the old place a good 'ol massive buff and shine. Our key administrative staff began moving from private, clean, new offices, to old, dirty, ugly corners and crevices. Many who had private spaces, would now be sharing offices or desks. No one complained. Everyone used the move as an opportunity to once again say "yes, first," and create something wonderful. As the owners and caretakers of the theatre, we felt blessed once again to be able to work with the greatest staff on the planet.

Jenni Lilledahl, Owner of the Brave New Workshop
Executive Director, Brave New Institute

Practical Applications:
What You Can Do Tomorrow

The path to innovation is a long, patient, inward journey. Remember, at the core of the Brave New Workshop is a group of individuals who have traveled down the path to their most creative self. Most of our work and products are created through an ensemble method, but like any good team, we are no better than any individual team member. For our team to be innovative, we must first be innovative individuals.

> The process will seem slow, especially at first, but you'll begin to see symptoms in your life. Usually the first one you notice is how much less time you spend judging, negating, and figuring out what is wrong with things. Say yes to that and celebrate it.

Although much of what has been discussed has been in terms of teams and groups and companies, it is important to note that every secret we share is easily applied to you as an individual. Say yes to yourself more, defer judgment in your own thoughts, realize that, like an improv scene, everything you need in your life truly already exists and is accessible to you.

Here are some practical exercises you can use to help embrace your own sense of creativity and innovation.

1. Honestly keep track of how many times you say yes to your own (or others') ideas and how many times you say no.

2. Seek out and appreciate innovative experiences in art, business, science, and nature.

3. Begin to participate in things you are uncomfortable with, things that scare you.

4. Watch kids play.

5. Announce at the next meeting you lead, that for he first 15 percent of the meeting, no one is allowed to judge any ideas generated.

6. Ask the people you lead to let you know how they are most comfortable communicating their ideas to you and to the group.

7. Record the symptoms you experience when you are feeling comfortable and creative, and conversely, how you feel when you're frustrated and unproductive. Try to increase the number of times you experience the positive symptoms.

8. Go through the funnel process *(see chapter 10)* by yourself with something risk free, such as a fictional sales proposal or a new product development.

9. Use the funnel process to write a short story or a poem.

10. Enroll in an improv class.

11. Make a list of uncommon and unpredicted events that have resulted in innovative successes in your workplace or home. Identify what mistakes have lead to innovation.

12. Have a conversation with someone without simultaneously preparing for your reply. Challenge yourself to do absolutely *nothing* but focus on the person you're listening to and try to remember every single word they said.

13. Ask the people on your team to communicate what they think is the worst possible outcome for a project, and then let them know that it is okay if that happens.

14. Change the channel on your TV without the remote control for one night and remember how ridiculous (and impossible) the idea of a wireless remote control must have seemed in 1978.

15. Ask your team to attempt to create a leaderless meeting, and then invite a stranger to join you for that meeting. See if the stranger can identify the leader of your group.

You can use our secrets to be your own innovative leader and to discover your own individual style of creativity. In forty-five years of improvisation, the Brave New Workshop has witnessed what happens when people decide to take action and incorporate these principles into their lives. All of the philosophies in the world won't increase innovation or productivity until someone internalizes them and takes action. Take action!

We're thankful for the stories that follow. These individuals are prime examples of how practicing the BNW secrets can positively affect your daily work life.

Student Testimonials

> *All people are creatively equal and creatively perfect.*

Gary Hestness
Vice President of Development, Hazelden Foundation

Because of the Brave New Workshop seminar I attended, there are several skills I believe I now apply at work every day. The exercises that we did in class gave me an opportunity to open my mind to new ideas. The process of letting go and trusting your own spontaneity is a critical skill in the fast paced environment of the workplace. I had one interesting observation in my class. There was a wide age range from my son who was nineteen years old to young adults in their 20s, serious improv students in their 30s and 40s, and a fairly large cohort of individuals 50 plus. I believe as we age, the ability to be spontaneous becomes less and less. Also, to trust one's own intuition becomes more difficult. We develop filters, screens, bias, and prejudice. These all play out in the workplace as we navigate the political landscape and manage and supervise employees in which a variety of supervisory styles are needed to get the work done. The younger group had no trouble with developing wacky, outrageous, and many times, very funny free floating skits and creative situations. It is that creativity that I believe over time can be hindered. For me, the improv classes created a new awareness about my rigidity and stiffness, and I also came to realize that through practice of improv there is a way to loosen yourself up. As this new awareness followed me to my workplace, I could see humor and spontaneity in every interaction. In turn trust and motivation occur with my peers and those who report to me.

I also think another very important improvement through my own interactions at work is that humor can be used to create a more interesting workplace and has the ability to create synergy and enjoyment in teams and workgroups. I can also see that as creative interdepartmental teams work together and are spontaneous, this enjoyment creates more creativity, motivation and a genuine bonding.

I think it is predictable as we spend time in our companies and organizations to fall into certain types of cultural habits and biases. The improvisation is an enjoyable way to question all the boundaries and status quo ways of doing business. For most organizations and businesses innovation and creativity are essential, but the perception is that there are no good tools out there to actually create cultural change. I would say that improvisational learning is a great tool for this purpose because it is experiential and integrates well for the adult learner.

Jim Kojis
Seventh Grade Teacher

My ability to teach seventh graders for the past twenty-three years has been enhanced by my improv training. The inherent randomness and unpredictability of adolescents tends to encourage a fluid approach to teaching. By having a relatively unscripted plan for the day, I'm able to adjust to the looniness caused by barometric changes, hormones, and post-Halloween hyperglycemia.

I used to prepare for travel by planning for all contingencies— mental plans for all emergencies, survival, and repair kits. It was very satisfying to dig into my repair kit and pull out cable ties, duct tape, or whatever. I found over time that it is impossible, of course, to prepare for everything. The frequent glitches that I wasn't prepared for were very frustrating. I felt as though I'd failed because my planning was inadequate.

My four years of improv training have taught me that as an improviser, I don't need to have a plan for everything. I can respond to any situation from the height of my intelligence.

I was brought up in the "if you want something done right, do it yourself" school. Trust in team members was a new concept for me. I always felt that it was up to me to come up with the creative idea or get the job done. I can remember vividly the moment in my improv training when I learned that I could rely on someone else. We were on stage and my scene partner made a declaration. I had nothing for her, and I knew it. She made another statement, I still had nothing helpful. She spoke again and I responded and we went on to create a really neat scene. As we left the stage, I realized that I wasn't alone and, more importantly, could rely on whomever I was performing with.

Improv principles such as honesty, trust, listening, and staying "in the moment" have really helped my work and personal life. I find it easier to deal with change. Improv helps me to deal with events that don't go according to the master plan and "surprises."

I had a very bad shoulder injury a couple of years ago. I couldn't use my left arm for three months. I was mad. My body failed me. I simply wanted my arm to be uninjured. I wanted not to have damaged it! I was getting depressed. It dawned on me to apply improv thinking to my problem. My shoulder was making a strong declaration—"I'm torn up and I don't work!" I was negating this declaration. I realized that I needed to "YES, AND!" it.

I said that yes, my shoulder is a mess and I need an operation and weeks to rehabilitate myself. After I came to this realization, my attitude improved almost immediately.

The world is a very random unpredictable place. I don't think that you can go through life with a plan or script. You just have to sort of make it up as you go along and improv has given me the tools to do that.

Sheila Simon
Director of Sales, Pixel Farm Inc./Pixel Farm Interactive

The philosophy of the "group mind" has enhanced my understanding and belief in its importance in our everyday lives. I have learned through my studies as a theologian (I have my MA in theology) as well as life experiences, how important creating a group mind within a community of any sort can do great good (as well as great evil). I cannot tell you how many times I have been in a rehearsal or on stage with my improv troupe when I have experienced this "mind connection" with my fellow troupe members. It is as if we are reading each other's minds. It is mystical. A true example of a group of people working (or playing) together to become "one mind." Hence when this improv philosophy is used for a greater good in other parts of one's life, be work, family, spiritual community, etc., we can see how the "group mind" can only enrich our lives and the world around us.

I found studying and performing improv helpful when I was making my career transitions in the recent past. Even though I have never been a shy or introverted person I was surprised to find how much improv study and performance helped me increase and expand even further on my courage and openness to exploring and trying new things. Not only have I changed careers during my time in studying improv, but my new found openness to exploration has gotten me into writing, performing, and producing comedy shows.

Studying and performing improv also increased my ability to sell better and do my job overall in a more productive way. Through "yes-anding" skills, I have increased my abilities to help a client explore their needs to give them the best solutions to their problems. And through "yes-anding," I have increased my ability to work better with my own staff. For example, in "yes-anding" your co-worker or client, you are not only able to affirm their contribution to a professional conversation, but are able to further explore ideas that you may never have explored. It forces you to really listen to each other and think positively about whatever is said. Responding positively to (in other words, "yes-anding") an idea, instead of immediately shooting it down, not only opens the group up to more possibilities than one may have imagined before, but also creates an atmosphere of trust and respect among your co-workers and/or clients. It helps remind us that every person has something important to say and contribute to each of our lives. We need to be open to hearing it and exploring it. Improv does just that.

Being forced to get out your comfort zone is important as a business professional. If you want to stay on top of your game and be open to all the changes that are going on in the world, both professionally and personally, you need to have the ability to have an open mind. So by learning the skills of improv to get you open to the bigger picture, you are actually listening and hearing others and remembering the importance of play in your life. You remember that it is through play that some of our most creative ideas come from.

Judith Froemming
College Design Instructor

When I started studying at the Brave New Institute, I had years of experience as a graphic designer and art director. I am also a trained teacher with a BFA.

Improv drew my attention primarily because I had a desire to improve on my presentation skills. A friend of mine kept telling me that I should take classes with the Brave New Workshop. I thought I'd be learning how to present myself more clearly and humorously. What I learned is that improv isn't jokes or gimmicks; it's about observing, telling the truth, and playing with the results. It's a daily practice. It's a good way to live your life.

The most valuable thing I'm learning, and which is taking me the longest to grasp, is to "Yes, and . . ." everything. It seems very simple, but much harder to live. Just when you think you've got it, you're negating again! But "Yes, and . . ." is my favorite. I've slowly become a better teacher, parent, partner, and friend. I have less to prove, and I don't need to be right anymore. I'm able to enter another's world and not be threatened that my world will collapse. Now I know what always was: We can create a new one as we go! There's no taking, only giving.

As a college design teacher, I find new students are often very attached to familiar ideas. One of my jobs is to teach them how to innovate: to create and recognize a "big idea." It was improv that actually helped me visualize that the most innovative ideas often surface from unlikely pairings of things and the willingness to create a new relationship between them.

Tim Erickson
Online Facilitator, www.politalk.com

My study of improvisation with the Brave New Workshop had a dramatic effect on how I deal with every day relationships and professional opportunities. I learned to "get out of my head" and "jump" or take chances. Most importantly, improvisation reinforced the importance of trusting myself, my instincts, and my colleagues. The Brave New Workshop approaches improvisation as a team activity and stresses the importance of relying on others. The increased trust that I put in my professional colleagues and partners, might be the single most valuable lesson that I took from improv.

Dennis Karlstad
CEO, Custom Business Video, Inc.

Improv is a big part of improvement. More than a year after being involved with the improv classes at the Brave New Institute, two big things have stayed with me and become part of myself. And I think they have improved my relationship with customers.

One is listening. We all do, sort of, but fifty-two weeks of practicing showed me how and when I wander as I listen. My interaction in class required that I sort of hang around the focused listening zone most of the time or risk blank stares when I responded. Beyond just the risk of embarrassment, I found my business and personal conversations became richer. I like that.

The other thing was learning about a part of me I had been uncomfortable with before. I don't know why or when I started being uncomfortable with not knowing what I was going to say or do next, but I was. The listening and response process taught at BNI led me through the dark horror of trying to think faster and faster so I knew what to say by the time the other person finished speaking.

I learned to trust that I had a response even when I didn't know what it was. How do I explain something like that? The net result was more time to listen. And my conversations became richer. I like that.

So, I can't report a 50 percent rise in sales because of BNI and improv but I can report a 100 percent improvement in personal and business conversations. And that builds better relationships.

I recommend BNW improv philosophy and practice for any level of any business.

Douglas Kilian
RF Engineer, T-Mobile, USA

The study of improvisational comedy has positively helped my career as an engineer. Improvisation teaches the student to react to comments and situations given, without pre-planning a response. In my daily work as an engineer, I've used this concept to keep an open mind with fellow colleagues. The concept of "gifting your partner" also has had an impact. It sets you up for a win-win relationship in a heated discussion, and helps build teamwork in the department. I have noticed that our weekly planning meetings seem more productive, and overall more enjoyable, since practicing these skills at the BNW weeks on end.

In addition to these simple ideas, taking improvisation lessons also helped me be more open with friends and co-workers. Most of the engineers I studied with and work with have a shy nature, and I am no exception.

By taking these classes, I have become more comfortable initiating conversations, and even using a declaration as a way to open up dialog. Sometimes the conversation does not go the direction I expected, or intended, but that's where other improvisation skills come to play.

Overall, the study of improvisational comedy has helped my career as an engineer develop, thanks to practicing those interpersonal skills that I had not worked on much in the past. It has increased my confidence in initiating and participating in conversations, and generally interacting with both the internal and external customers of my department. Thank you, Brave New Workshop!!

Bernard Armada, Ph.D.

Chair & Assistant Professor Communication Studies Department, University of St. Thomas

Perhaps the most important gift I have received from studying improvisation is the ability to think outside the box and discover innovative solutions to personal or professional problems. Every human being possesses this skill, but studying improv on a weekly basis has allowed me to be mindful of my capacity to use it. I have come to view improvisation almost as a form of therapy or religion. Many people go to church or synagogue to strengthen their spirit and be reminded of the need to do good in the world. In a similar way, weekly improv classes remind me to practice a number of principles that are effective in personal/professional life, as well as on the stage. Some of these principles are: (1) support the people with whom you work—make them look like geniuses whenever possible; (2) avoid dominating others by trying to steal the spotlight; (3) allow things to unfold organically rather than attempting to control the outcome; and (4) trust your teammates, no matter what, and make yourself worthy of their trust.

As far as philosophy goes, improv always reminds me of the words of my undergraduate mentor who made me want to pursue a PhD and teach in the humanities: "Man is at his best when he is thoughtful, careful, and touched by good humor." Every time I pass through the doors of the Brave New Workshop I find myself surrounded by people who exemplify my mentor's words and who encourage me to be a better human being.

As a college professor, studying improv has improved my work life in countless ways. Here are a few.

1. A much stronger ability to think on my feet.

2. A much stronger ability to connect with undergraduates.

3. Better listening skills.

4. Greater confidence in front of the class.

5. An incredible new repertoire of teaching resources in terms of examples and classroom exercises.

6. A much stronger ability to facilitate cohesion among colleagues.

7. A much stronger ability to facilitate group interactions.

8. A much greater willingness to take risks.

9. Most important, a tendency to see the workplace as a positive, playful environment in which colleagues may enjoy each other's company without losing productivity.

In many ways, improv is similar to the "Fish!" philosophy that has become popular in so many organizational settings. The big difference, however, is that by studying improv, one has the opportunity, literally, to practice what he/she preaches.

Studying improvisation is important for anyone interested in personal or professional growth. I cannot stress this enough. On my way home from my very first improv class, I remember calling my wife and saying, "You have to take a class! You'll learn so much about your own interpersonal communication skills." I am so thankful for having taken improv classes because I believe improvisation is a metaphor for life. Although this may seem ridiculous to an outsider, improvisation brings out the experiences that make for fulfilling personal and professional lives: good humor, spontaneity, risk, mutual respect, trust, support, openness to others, acceptance, self-esteem, creativity, togetherness, and problem solving abilities. Also, one does not have to be "a ham" or love the spotlight to be a good improviser. In fact, those who think they're funny often are in for a rude awakening when they've got to learn to share the spotlight with others, or even sacrifice their own "glory" for the success of the group. One can participate at any age or skill level—emphasis is placed on spontaneity, listening, and working with others rather than on one's individual ability to make others laugh.

Our Creative Funnel Process

The Idea Generation Process of the Brave New Workshop (The Funnel)

The Brave New Workshop uses the funnel process to create our mainstage show products as well as corporate comedy scripts, thematic ideas for corporate events, and our customized training programs. In fact, we use the funnel process for almost every project and product development initiative throughout the company—regardless of length—from a five-minute brainstorming session to a three-year implementation of a strategic plan.

The example we use to illustrate the funnel process is the development of our most traditional and well-known product. That product is a one-hour and forty-five minute written script performed on our main stage in Minneapolis, Minnesota. In a matter of fifty-six days of work, eight show team members begin with one word of inspiration, and then execute the funnel process that ultimately leads to our opening night performance.

Like any manufacturing company, we work hard at creating assurances that the quality of our product is consistent and reliable. We also experience the typical challenges of maintaining that quality over time. In our case, those challenges are things like talent and experience of actors and writers, the political climate that exists in the country during the time of our production, and perhaps what popular icons are in or out of fashion. Because we have so many variables and such a long history of quality, we realize the only real assurance in the end result of our work is that we strictly adhere to our idea generation process. Diligently executing the steps in the funnel process has proven to be much more

123

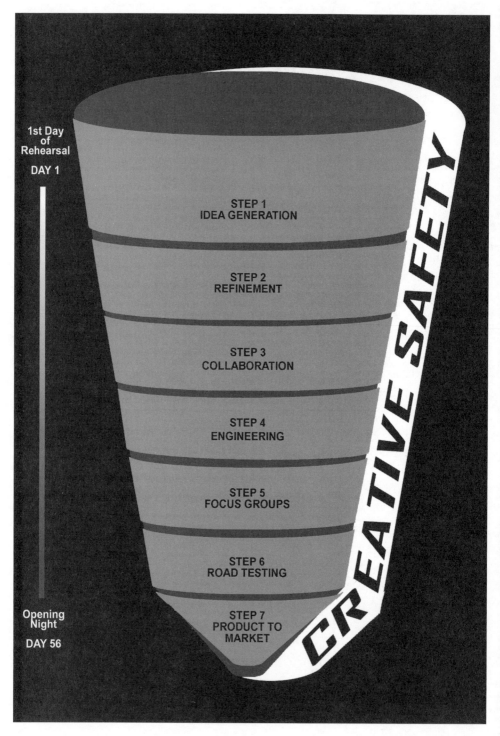

Innovation at the Speed of Laughter

reliable than stumbling on a brilliant idea, a talented actor, or the right market conditions.

Step 1—Idea Generation

> *Seven people create six hundred one-sentence ideas in seventy-two hours.*

The focus of our first step is "volume." We understand that it is the quantity of ideas that is important, not necessarily the quality or the ability to implement them. We consider ourselves "mass producers" at this point, and pay no attention to the perceived value of an idea. We simply need to produce as many ideas as we can, as fast as we can.

The mass production of ideas at this point in our process reinforces our belief that great ideas are rarely ever created in their implementable form. Several dozen, perhaps hundreds, of ideas must be created in order to produce a single viable and profitable idea.

For our product, which typically requires twenty-five sketches or songs to make up our opening night script, we found we need to produce six hundred one-sentence ideas. The ratio of 24 to 1 seems to produce a consistently innovative product for our manufacturing process. We encourage you to find the ratio that works for your individual needs.

The beginning of our process is the introduction of a word or phrase to be used as inspiration for the overall theme of the show. This word or phrase is simply our jumping off point. It represents a concise definition of a theme that is of topical interest to our audience. This theme is often an inspiration for the title of the show—something the BNW is well known for. As you can see from the following list of titles and corresponding themes, our titles are often a barometer of what was happening in America at the time.

- "I Compute, Therefore IBM" (1983—the computerization of America)

- "Yuppie See, Yuppie Do" (1985—excessiveness)

- "The Viceman Cometh" (1986–addiction)
- "Prozac: It's What's for Dinner, or Let the Side Effects Begin" (2000–the answer is to medicate)
- "I'm Okay, You're a Jerk" (1981–self help)
- "Victim Nation: The Don't Blame Me Revue" (1994–responsibility)
- "Cinderella and the Glass Ceiling" (1994–women in the workplace)
- "Saving Clinton's Privates, or Swallow the Leader" (1998–need we say?)
- "Martha Stewart, Prison Vixen" (2003–entitlement)

Once the theme is announced, idea generation begins. We compare it to Jiffy Pop popcorn because of the speed and exponential quality of our productivity. It looks like a group of people casually sitting in a comfortable environment with two other people typing as fast as they can in order to make sure all the ideas are recorded.

To create the six hundred one-sentence ideas, it typically takes three eight-hour "stream of consciousness" brainstorming sessions. We refer to these six hundred ideas as "The Master Inspiration List."

The Master Inspiration List is used throughout the entire 56-day funnel process. Each team member uses it as a reference point. It can also serve as a way for those team members to recall the energy and excitement of the first three days of rehearsal, and to help keep the ideas fresh throughout the process.

To achieve this volume of ideas and idea generation speed, we must adhere to the 8 Secrets contained within this book. The secret that is most essential for this specific step is the secret of Deferring Judgment (chapter 2).

Step 2—Refinement

Each team member is asked to take responsibility for twenty to twenty-five ideas and place their initials next to these ideas on the Master Inspiration List. They are encouraged to choose the ideas they are most passionate about exploring further or that elicit outrage within them. In other words, the ones that get them the most fired up.

> • Team members declare accountability for the twenty to twenty-five ideas they are most passionate about.
>
> • The team must recognize, accept, and promote the concept that individuals will approach ideas differently and communicate them to the group in their own style.

Once assigned, the team members immediately begin to work on the next tangible product of the process, the Key Elements. The purpose of the Key Elements is to simply create a format so that the essential ingredients of the product can be recorded, organized, and understood. Over the years, we found that the simple step of idea organization was a huge stumbling block. Our writers would simply let the idea slip away into oblivion if they were not able to succinctly communicate the components that made up their idea. By creating a simple worksheet and format for our team members to follow and complete, we discovered the right blend of innovation and organization.

We ask the team members to identify and thoroughly define the most essential building blocks of the product—in our case, a comedy sketch. For our purposes, those building blocks are (1) the satirical point, (2) a description of the characters, (3) the action points of the scene, (4) a thorough description of the environment in which the scene will take place, and (5) a personal explanation of why they believe the idea is funny.

In our process, individuals are not necessarily required to compile all five aspects of the Key Elements into a sketch worksheet. It is often acceptable and encouraged for each of the team members to present a partially completed Key Element worksheet to the group. This relieves the pressure from that idea's author and allows everyone to begin a collaborative and multi-point of view approach to each idea. Deferring Judgment still plays an important role in this stage of the process, as we are in the infancy of that idea's development.

The secret that is most essential to this step is the secret of Sharing Focus and Accepting All Styles *(chapter 3)*. At this point, each individual will approach the Key Elements in his or her own unique way and communicate their idea in their own unique style. Although we have a standardized vehicle of organization and communication, we also support the sharing of focus and acceptance of all styles as a way to ensure that every team member can create and communicate ideas in a way that is most comfortable for them.

Step 3—Collaboration

As individual team members work to complete the sketch worksheets for the ideas they have chosen, our process enters its next phase. This phase of collaboration typically lasts for two weeks. Team members present completed, or incomplete, sketch worksheets, one idea at a time. They can present them orally and/or distribute a hard copy. Once the worksheet is presented to the group, a discussion takes place that involves both critique and new idea generation.

A critical tool we have developed, and use with diligence and discipline, is a very specific vocabulary to discuss and critique team members'

- *No one person is responsible for the completion of the Key Elements. They are simply responsible for helping to move this idea through this part of the process.*
- *When we practice the secret of "Yes, First!" by saying "yes, and" to each other and to each other's ideas, we are able to explode the process and explore all the possibilities that may exist for an idea.*

Key Elements. By using a vocabulary that clearly separates the work from the individual, we have been able to achieve an environment in which the group can improve the current set of Key Elements. Additionally, they can offer new ideas without apprehension or worry about hurting anyone's feelings.

Other tools that are used to improve and complete the Key Elements for an idea are:

1. Ideas are improvised on stage by the entire team. The beta version of this concept is executed in several different ways by the improvisers. This "working on our feet" process allows us to look at the idea differently, or find a specific aspect of the Key Elements that was not apparent through typical group discussion.

2. Oftentimes, we will examine whether or not the specific Key Element we are trying to complete would perhaps be better served if it was incorporated or combined with another Master Inspiration List idea or Key Element currently being explored.

We are very conscious at this point in the process that certain ideas can organically lose their ability to make us passionate about them. And so, because we are still in the widest point of the funnel and still concerned with quantity and not quality, we embrace the option that perhaps it is simply better to move on to the next idea and eliminate this one, or put it on the proverbial back burner. Because we always maintain a copy of the Master Inspiration List and any Key Elements started, we will often find ourselves discovering a different use for an idea later in the process.

Once the entire group has had the opportunity to provide input on the Key Elements of an idea and the sketch worksheet has been completed, the group—and ultimately the director—decides whether the idea is ready for the next step or needs to be set aside for now.

This is the first point in our creative process in which the director begins to act as editor and takes responsibility for deciding which ideas will continue through the funnel process. It also qualifies ideas to enter the next step, Engineering, and the creation of the first draft script.

The secret that is most essential to this step is the secret of "Yes, First!" *(chapter 7)*. At this point in the process we are in the mode of idea explosion. We need to take the idea that we are working on in its most raw and simple form, and say yes to its potential, its growth, and to the rest of the group. We have learned that the simple practice of saying the words "yes, and" allows us to take a one-sentence version of an idea and inflate it into a thoroughly fleshed out Key Element or idea. When we are really practicing the secret of "Yes, First!" in this part of this process, it looks like those capsules you put in your tub and add water. Thirty seconds later they are a two-foot in diameter sponge dinosaur. I'm sure that's exactly what it will seem like to you.

Step 4—Engineering

The individuals who are accountable for the ideas they chose from the Master Inspiration List will now begin to transform the Key Elements into a first draft of a script. These script drafts are presented to the group and read out loud. Often times, we read them on stage and on our feet as a way to involve our bodies and ensure the pacing and energy needed in reading the script is present.

After the script is "performed" for the first time, the group members discuss how they feel about the script, making sure they use specific vocabulary separating the work from the person. Since the individuals in the group are discussing, making observations, and sometimes critiquing another team member's work, we are very conscious of maintaining an environ-

- *Scripts are read aloud.*
- *Group observations are made.*
- *Director makes revision decisions.*
- *People feel safe to express their opinions.*
- *Reduced drama = increased productivity.*

ment that does not create negative stimulus for either the author or peer critics. You will hear terms such as "pace" or "intensity," "the need for resolution," "heightening," "redundancy," "the need for specificity," and similar terms that are emotionless and clearly attached to the document and not the author.

After group members make their observations and facilitate discussion, the director decides what changes or additions need to be made in that version of the script. The script change recommendations are the author's homework and are usually done outside the rehearsal process. This read-discuss-revise process lasts all the way until opening night and many sketches are rewritten more than five times before they reach their final form. This is the first point in the process in which we begin to evaluate whether or not the sketch becomes part of our final product. Typically, we write first drafts for approximately sixty Key Elements and only about twenty-five make it to the stage as a completed sketch and part of the product we bring to market.

As the scripts become more and more refined, the director begins to change his view from seeing them as individual pieces to considering the relationship they might have with each other. He or she examines how they may be organized in a way that will create a successful show. At the end of this phase, the director may have even gone so far as to create his or her first draft of a "running order" or show outline.

Another common practice at this stage in our creative process is that we purposely transfer the ownership and responsibility of the idea to another team member. We do this in order to get a new perspective and approach.

The secret that is most essential to this step is to Create a Statusless Environment *(chapter 5)*. We need to ensure that both the author of the individual script, and the team members who critique it, feel creatively safe at this point in the process. In order for the team to truly achieve a level of dialogue that is without reservation or kind bias, everyone in the group must feel comfortable and safe to speak freely and communicate bluntly. Because we drastically reduce the amount of classic office drama, we increase the speed at which we refine our product.

Step 5—Focus Groups

One of the wonderful luxuries of the live theatre business is we have a focus group consisting of actual customers every time we perform a show. We are able to extract customer satisfaction information and test our next product in real time with real customers.

We maximize this nightly focus group by performing the scripts we are working on for show "B" for the audience that just watched show "A." After show "A" takes its bow, the director takes the stage and tells the audience that tonight they will have the opportunity to see some "works in progress" from the new show we are writing. The director informs the audience that the actors will have scripts in hand and will not be accompanied by the props and costumes that may eventually be used in the scene. Because our theatre is in Minnesota and often filled with very passive and stoically nice individuals, we have to aggressively prompt the audience to give honest and audible reactions. We let them know they are part of our process and we appreciate their input as a way to provide them with the best possible comedy we can produce.

- *We perform our work in progress for the audience.*
- *We now share focus with them and listen to their reaction.*
- *We leave our egos on the stage.*

While the script is performed, the director and cast members who are not performing watch the action on stage and the audience's reaction. They gather volumes of information from the customers regarding the content, pace, delivery, and tone of the product being tested. The audience responses are noted in detail and used to refine the script and determine whether (1) it needs to be shorter, (2) it needs to end differently, (3) a character needs to be removed, (4) the material is appropriate for an entire sketch, or (5) two sketches should be combined into one.

This is the first part of our process where market constraints begin to show themselves. For every show, there are sketches in which our customers do not necessarily share the team's opinion of the quality of the product. In these cases, the scripts sometimes need to be drastically changed or eliminated. Because we produced so many ideas at the beginning of our funnel process, we do not have to "go back to the drawing board," we simply have to refocus our energies, for example, on script forty-two instead of script thirty-six.

The secret that is most essential to this step is Sharing Focus and Accepting All Styles *(chapter 3)*. We now begin to share focus with our new team member, the audience. We focus our eyes and ears toward our customers. We watch and listen not only for their laughter or applause, but keenly observe their attention span, their body language, and their fidgetiness. We also listen without egos. There is an endless list of theatres that no longer exist because it was clear to them their audience was "wrong."

Step 6—Road Testing

At this step, we are eight days from opening night. The actors lovingly refer to this period of time as "hell week." We have created an opening and closing number. We have incorporated transitions between our sketches and songs. We have re-set the lights in our theatre, designed and constructed costumes and props, memorized our lines, and learned our choreography and blocking. Now it's time to truly see if this ship floats.

Typically, the director narrows down the scripts to approximately two hours worth of material, of which fifteen to

> • *From concept car to the dealership floor in eight days.*
>
> • *If we don't change, we don't meet our customers' expectations.*

twenty minutes will be "cut" during the next seven days. The director also creates a running order of scripts that is likely to be altered after each of the five preview week performances.

This is the first time our customers are exposed to our new product in its fully rehearsed and polished form. This step in the funnel is challenging because we have a short period of time to change many things: we are always performing one show while writing another, there is often crossover within the cast (some members of the current show are also in the new show), and we typically open the new show one weekend after we close the current show. Our average show run varies from twelve to sixteen weeks. We have created a situation that most theatres, and certainly most traditional manufacturing companies, would definitely find unreasonable and probably impossible. Although this self-created obstacle presents swift challenges, it is one of the most important characteristics of our work that differentiates us from our competition. It also creates a sense of urgency that we believe drives our creativity.

This part of the process is difficult for the team. They are tired and have a tendency to begin to doubt the quality of their product. Like all of us at times, they would rather be "done" than re-work the show yet again. Each night after preview performances, we make drastic changes in the sketch line-up and the casting and are still determining which scripts to include. Each day following preview performances, we rehearse a new version of the show from start to finish, and then perform that new product for the next night's audience. After the final preview performance, and more than fifty days of hard work, we have finally refined our product in a way that is most attractive to our customers. We are ready for opening night.

The secret that is most essential to this step is Perceiving Change as Fuel *(chapter 8)*. Just when we think we are close to completion and things will become more consistent and predictable, preview week begins. There is no doubt that the immense changes that happen within this short period of the funnel process drastically increase our workload. Unlike many work places, we actually welcome these changes because we realize the magnitude of their importance in producing a product that meets our customers' expectations. Oftentimes these changes also provide insight for our actors that would not have happened if we had simply settled for a product that was easy to perform or "generally acceptable" to our audience. The expectation we have set with our customers over the last forty-five years is that each new show will be better than the last. We need to live up to our reputation for cutting-edge satirical comedy theatre.

Step 7—Product to Market

Six hundred ideas, one hundred Key Elements, sixty first drafts of scripts, fifty-six days of rehearsal, eight team members, five nights of previews, and it all comes down to this one night.

To put our product in perspective from a manufacturing standpoint, the actual amount of material we perform on opening night is equal to five episodes of a prime-time sitcom. Oh, and by the way, it's live—we only have one shot.

Like any small company producing its own product, opening night brings up anxieties and questions like "will they like it?" or perhaps, more importantly, "will they like it enough to pay for it?" As one of the few completely self-sustaining theatres in the country, we are intimately aware of the relationship between ticket sales and profitability. During some years, it was the relationship between ticket sales and existence.

When we bring our product to market on opening night, there are typically four to six theatre critics in the audience. The difference between positive or negative reviews has the potential to affect ticket sales and revenues by 40 to 50 percent over a 12-week run of the show.

> - *Energy of the team has moved from free-flowing creativity to high-pressure productivity.*
> - *The entire process will be judged by the result of one night.*
> - *The critics (industry analysts) can significantly influence a twelve-week revenue period.*

As we arrive at the bottom of our funnel process on opening night, there is a drastic increase in the tension and energy of our team, compared to the first day of rehearsal. There is tremendous pressure on our cast to perform at a level that meets the standards of our company and lives up to our reputation. We are also very cognizant that we need to generate next week's ticket sales.

So where does the confidence in our product come from? Is it in the individual talents of the team members? Perhaps. Is it the trust the team has in the director? Maybe. Mostly this confidence is found in the well-proven and consistent outcome that our creative funnel process ensures.

Remember, our shows typically run for a twelve to sixteen week period. We encourage the team to continually discover new ways to improve the product during the show's lifespan. We use a specific process of nightly evaluation to discover new and innovative ways to improve the product. We found that a team member's level of commitment to improve the product is directly related to the amount of ownership they had in the actual creation of that product.

The secret that is most essential to this step is Declarations *(chapter 4)*. Our team is responsible for manufacturing the product *and* "delivering" it to our customers; therefore, we need to promote their skills of confidence, stage presence, and declarative behavior. In our product delivery, there is a drastic difference in simply "presenting it" to the audience and "performing it" before the audience. Without being arrogant, we need to have our team hit the stage and deliver the material in a way that says, "we are excited and proud of our product, and you should be too." This declarative style of delivery is sometimes referred to as salesmanship.

Summary

I would like to say that our creative process was born out of insight and brilliance, but the truth is, it is a result of necessity and survival. Like many innovative manufacturing firms, we have unique challenges that are specific to our product:

1. Every show is an original piece of work created by our team;
2. The constraints of our product-to-market schedule (we are always creating one show while we are performing another);
3. A very limited market testing period; and
4. A tremendous amount of pressure to create a product that lives up to our forty-five year reputation for innovative, cutting-edge comedy.

In order to create an innovative product within the above parameters, we have had to develop consistency in a manufacturing process filled with variables. The process is so important and has produced such a proven product, that it is revered and respected by our team members and rarely challenged. When outsiders ask, "How have you been able to create a fresh and marketable product through the conservative 50s, the turbulent 60s, the psychedelic 70s, the excessive 80s, the apathetic 90s, and the unpredictable new millennium?" We reply, "We follow the funnel."

So perhaps at this point you're saying, "Wow, sounds like a cool process, good for you, but unfortunately, I don't work in a company that produces comedy scripts. I work in a company that manages real estate assets or creates business insurance programs or develops new database system applications or . . ." Seven years ago, I had the same perspective and wasn't convinced, let alone clear, that our funnel process could be applied to other industries and work cultures. Since then, I have shared our process with hundreds of corporate clients. They have successfully adapted it and implemented it into their own culture, and the results I have witnessed have been remarkable. I am thoroughly convinced our process is applicable to any group of people who want to find the next great idea.

The Brave New Workshop
Yesterday & Today

Since 1958, our theatre has played a unique role within the community in which it exists. Our contrarian, progressive, and often times irreverent, product has found a niche in a community that prides itself on reliable conservatism. We are a theatre that exposes and comments on things that most Minnesotans think about, but rarely talk about. Most of what we do today is simply an extension of our founder's insight and intelligent sense of mischief. To help you clearly understand who the Brave New Workshop is, here is a brief history of how the BNW came to be:

Historical Timeline

1932 Dudley Riggs is born in Little Rock, Arkansas. He joins his family's circus as a performer at age five.

1950s The advent of television causes the attendance of live performances to wane. Dudley and some of his fellow circus performers bring a new act to New York City, incorporating "audience input" into parts of the show for the first time. Calling themselves the "Instant Theatre Company," the group brings the show to Chicago, Washington, D.C. and Burbank, California, before settling in Minneapolis.

1958 Dudley brings his "Instant Theatre Company" to the Café Espresso on University Avenue in Northeast Minneapolis. His café/theatre houses the United States' first espresso machine west of the Mississippi.

1961   The current style of comedy satire/satire revue shows is established, and the name "Brave New Workshop" is added.

1962   The first improv classes are taught to high school students at the BNW.

1965   After mounting productions in the Café Espresso on University Avenue, then moving to 207 East Hennepin Avenue, Dudley and crew follow the muse to 2605 Hennepin Avenue on November 30, 1965, making the former bike shop into their permanent home. The ticket price of a BNW show in 1965 is $2. Current owners John Sweeney and Jenni Lilledahl are born.

1970   BNW International Touring Company is formed to take the BNW style of improvisation to college campuses and outlying Minnesota communities, as well as to other states and countries.

1971   Dudley opens a second theatre, the Experimental Theater Company (ETC), at 1430 Washington Avenue in the Seven Corners area of Minneapolis. This theatre and café become home to other BNW productions, as well as stand-up comedy and variety acts. The 2605 Hennepin location continues to be the theatre's main stage. Dudley operates the ETC until 1991, when he consolidates his operations back to the single 2605 Hennepin location.

Mid-1970s   The BNW International Touring Company expands to include performances at conventions and for private businesses. This is the first time the BNW crosses over from stage to boardroom.

1975   The fourth annual New Year's Eve Party at the BNW features a three-and-a-half-hour satirical comedy focusing on the low points of the year, as well as a buffet for the grand price of $8.50.

1990   The BNW celebrates twenty-five years at 2605 Hennepin by reducing ticket prices to the 1965 price of $2.

1997   John Sweeney and Jenni Lilledahl purchase the theatre from its founder, Dudley Riggs. The name of the historic theatre changes slightly to "The Brave New Workshop, founded by Dudley Riggs in 1958."

1997   The BNW signs a seven-figure contract to be the official comedy provider for the new Disney Cruise Line ships, the Magic and the Wonder.

1997   The BNW decides to aggressively expand its corporate services division, developing new corporate entertainment and training products and increasing its scope from less than fifteen events per year to more than one hundred.

1998   The BNW celebrates its forty-year anniversary by opening a new space for the theatre's main stage and offices at 3001 Hennepin Avenue in Calhoun Square.

1999   The Brave New Institute grows from seven students to a school hosting more than two hundred fifty students each week. It now has eleven teachers and fifteen sections of class per week.

2000   The Brave New Workshop produces "Flanagan's Wake," an interactive Irish comedy at the 2605 Hennepin location. This production is in cooperation with the Noble Fool Theatre of Chicago.

2001   The BNW reaches another milestone when, for the first time in its history, it opens a theatre in a location other than Minneapolis. The BNW renovates the historic

Palace Theatre at 17 West Seventh Place. In January 2001, the BNW opens that space with the Irish comedy, "Flanagan's Wake."

2002   The BNW moves its main stage operations back to the 2605 Hennepin Avenue theatre, once again establishing this location as its historic home.

2003   "Flanagan's Wake" closes after a successful two-year run, making way for "MN: It's Not Just For Lutherans Anymore!" which opens in the Palace Theatre space September 5.

2004   Despite a poor economy, the Brave New Workshop continues to operate two theatres in the Twin Cities, an improvisational school of nearly three hundred students, and a corporate services division with a reputation as a national leader in corporate entertainment, training, and keynote speeches.

Our Motto

Promiscuous Hostility, Positive Neutrality

"Our motto is evoked in everything that we do. 'Presenting new ideas,' 'milking sacred cows,' and 'puncturing pomposity' is the underlying theme of 'promiscuous hostility.' We have covered virtually every issue that has made headlines—and brought some little-known controversies to the forefront. However, improv is thought to be, by nature, liberal because it is freethinking. But because of the left-wing tendencies in the early days, we wanted to be sure to always explore both sides of the spectrum, thus the addition of 'positive neutrality.'"

Dudley Riggs, founder, Brave New Workshop Comedy Theatre

Our Mission

The Brave New Workshop is a comedy theatre, which exposes, illuminates, and celebrates the obsessions and inconsistencies in society. The Brave New Workshop is a writer's theatre, a theatre of ideas. The Brave New Workshop is an actor's theatre, a theatre of emotion and spontaneity. The Brave New Workshop is an instant theatre, a theatre of immediate response, dedicated to entertainment, education, and play.

Our Products

Brave New Workshop Comedy Theatre

The Brave New Workshop Theatre is the oldest, satirical comedy theatre in the country. Dudley Riggs brought his "Instant Theatre Company" performances to Minneapolis in the mid-1950s. Originally called "trunk shows," Dudley and other performers created unique theatre performances based completely on audience suggestions every single night using costumes and props they stored in a trunk on stage. More than forty-five years later, we're still producing this same basic style of show, using very few props and costumes, on an essentially bare stage.

As of this printing, hundreds of talented writer/actors have passed through our doors, and have created approximately 247 shows of original sketch comedy for the BNW stage. Each and every sketch was developed using some version of the creative process outlined in this book. The 8 Secrets that were outlined in previous chapters have been present in our theatre since its beginning. Since President Truman, we have consistently produced some of the most stellar improvisation-based sketch comedy in the world. Here is a sampling of some of our most memorable show titles:

1. Morals is a Six-Letter Word (1963)
2. The All Dirty Revue (A Study in Quiet Good Taste) (1966)
3. The Race Riot Revue: Hate is a Summer Festival (1967)
4. Charlie! or, Manson Ate Grapes (1970)
5. Ripped off the Cross! The Last Crusade of Billy B'Jesus (1973)
6. Atheism Means Never Having to Say You're Lutheran (1978)
7. Prairie Island Home Companion, or the Return to the Nuclear Family (1980)
8. National Velveeta, or What a Friend We Have in Cheeses (1980)

> - *Founded in 1958 by Dudley Riggs, a fifth generation Barnum & Bailey Circus performer and one of the pioneers of improvisational theatre*
> - *The nation's longest running satirical comedy theatre*
> - *Produces world class comedy shows in its theatres in Minneapolis and Saint Paul*
> - *Has performed its innovative, message driven comedy for over three million people*
> - *Has spawned the careers of hundreds of Hollywood actors and writers*
> - *A Minnesota institution*

9. Aging Bull, or Sex and the Senile Citizen (1982)

10. I Compute, Therefore IBM (1983)

11. All Stressed Up with No Place to Go (1985)

12. Fixing Men—A Women's Guide to Home Repair (1987)

13. The Way We War—Vietnam! The Musical (1987)

14. Don't Worry, Be Stupid (1989)

15. Censorship of Fools, or Jesse at the Helm (1990)

16. Bushwhacked I: The Recession Follies (1992)

17. Politically Correct Means Always Having to Say You Are Sorry (1993)

18. No Newt is Good Newt: The Congressional Follies (1995)

19. Viagra! The Second Coming (1998)

20. Prozac, It's What's for Dinner, or Let the Side Effects Begin (2000)

21. Bushwhacked II: One Nation Under Stress (2002)

22. Total Recall 2: The Governator (2003)

23. Das Bootylicious, or Women of Mass Destruction (2004)

24. Electile Dysfunction; or Two Johns, a Dick, and a Bush (2004)

Brave New Institute

After clearly defining our role as a cutting-edge creator of satirical comedy, our audiences began to ask if we could teach them the art of improvisation. As we began to share the history and philosophies of the BNW, the Brave New Institute was born. This led to the formal creation of our school. Over the years, that instructional part of our company has ebbed and flowed, going from casual improvisational "drop-ins" to our current eighteen-month curriculum. Along the way, we have accumulated, refined, and maximized the insights of the hundreds of actors and instructors who have expanded on Dudley's original improvisational model.

Today, the Brave New Institute welcomes more than two hundred fifty students into its classrooms each week to explore the incredible improv principles and philosophies outlined in this book. Additionally, the elements of creative safety, self-confidence, listening, and cooperation are utilized in several community outreach and youth programs directed by the instructors of the BNI.

- *The educational division of the Brave New Workshop Comedy Theatre*
- *Recognized as a premier improvisational training center*
- *Teaches the principles and philosophies of the BNW's unique brand of improvisation*
- *Offers an eighteen-month, five-level curriculum*
- *Educates more than two hundred fifty adult students each week*
- *Conducts outreach in youth programs throughout Twin Cities' communities*
- *Developed and refined more than one hundred fifty improvisational exercises over the last forty-five years*
- *Boasts an 82 percent retention and graduation rate in a student population comprised of 30 percent actors and 70 percent business professionals*

Brave New Workshop Corporate Services Division

A third product line begged to be created in the early 1970s, as members of our audience began to request that our creative staff develop and perform business theatre sketches and songs for events outside the walls of our theatre. Those early shows were the beginning of what is now the most profitable division within our organization, our corporate services division. This wonderful by-product of our original mission allows us to continue as a self-sustaining organization. Unlike most other arts organizations, we do not rely on federal funding or contributions. Currently, the corporate services division creates, produces, and performs more than one hundred corporate entertainment events per year.

In addition to providing clients with corporate entertainment, we have developed a world-class corporate training program. As the scope of our school drastically increased in the late 1990s under the guidance of Executive Director Jenni Lilledahl, this newest corporate product reared its profitable head. It became apparent that the fundamentals of improvisation were beneficial to many people, actors and non-actors alike. In response to the discovery

- *Uses improvisational-based training to increase the skill sets of employees of local, regional, national, and international corporations, including the highest level of executive training for dozens of Fortune 100 companies*
- *Utilizes a combination of lecture, interactive/experiential exercises, and facilitated group discussion*
- *Employs participatory group based exercises which have been tested for years in the Brave New Institute and refined to meet the needs of the corporate culture*
- *Uses a Liberal Arts learning model approach to help participants gain insights about common issues by having an uncommon experience*
- *Conducts more than one hundred training sessions per year worldwide*
- *Boasts a 70 percent repeat client rate*

> *Our corporate training and entertainment programs grew 400 percent in eighteen months.*

of this market condition, we refined our curriculum to meet the needs of the corporate world. It has become our everlasting gob stopper.

Since 1998, the BNW has consistently provided corporate improvisational training as a way to increase the innovation, teambuilding, acceptance of change, and leadership capabilities of the corporate world. Participants describe our corporate training as "innovative," "groundbreaking," "shocking," and an "outward bound for the mind." We attribute our success to the very nature of improvisation and our ability to help people learn commonly understood principles through an uncommon experience.

Our Culture

In Practice Every Day

Much like an improvisational scene, the humble declaration that Dudley made in 1958, was met with a "yes, first" then expanded, fueled with energy and hard work. For all these years, the employees of the Brave New Workshop have utilized the 8 Secrets to transform a single, wonderful idea into a rather large and diverse company.

Undeniably, our history and philosophies have brought us to where we are today, employing all of the secrets of improvisation to run our business. We are not unrealistic about the challenges of making a small budget, self-sustaining theatre successful. By practicing the secrets of improvisation, we have been able to create an uncommonly positive and innovative workplace.

Every day, in every aspect and every division of our "idea factory," we respect and practice the secrets. The following are examples of how we apply the unique secrets of the BNW to affect the more traditional areas of managing our company. So far, it seems to be working pretty well.

Recruitment

We are constantly being asked the question, "Where do you find such wonderful people to work for the Brave New Workshop?" We have never had a problem finding qualified—and typically overqualified—employees. Our hiring practice is to focus on the recruitment of quality individuals, not necessarily the individuals who possess the best skills for the position.

When interviewing potential employees, we let every prospect know that, if hired, their ideas will be respected, and we will provide a statusless environment. We also let them know that they will be encouraged and safe to be their most original selves. Many BNW employees have chosen to leave traditional corporate positions in pursuit of an environment that will challenge, empower, and excite them. They desire to be surrounded by conscientious, intelligent, vibrant, and passionate people. Our employees tend to be willing to commit and contribute to our mission, despite the fact that our compensation package is typically one-half of a comparable corporate position. They simply love what they do.

And that's why a Harvard graduate spends sixty-five hours a week, sharing an office in the basement of a building that floods and smells like skunk butt for $23,000 a year.

Retention

We allow employees to constantly evaluate and reevaluate how passionate they are about their specific job descriptions. We allow them to re-create their job description as often as needed to ensure they are excited and motivated every day.

Employees are held accountable to themselves and the team—or in our words "to the scene"—not to management's expectations. When a team member is not meeting expectations, such as following through on a declared objective, the team lets them know their current performance is below team standards.

We have no vacation policy, the amount of days our employees choose not to work is completely up to them. We simply ask everyone to balance his or her work and personal life. We want them to do their job to the best of their ability, and stay with the company as long as possible.

As a result of this, one of the best corporate training instructors in the country, BNW's artistic director Caleb McEwen, will soon focus solely on directing our stage productions because that's his passion. Our director of finance has been with the company eighteen years.

Policy Setting

Like good improvisation, we do not have many policies that are set in stone. Instead, we have guidelines, standards, and beliefs by which we create expectations of conduct and productivity.

Perhaps the most important "policy" is that all ideas and points of view are respected. This often shows itself in weekly staff meetings or quarterly strategic planning meetings. Frequently individuals will state a point of view that is drastically different from that of management's or perhaps even the majority of the employees. Instead of judging the individual, the group simply acknowledges and appreciates that the perspective has added another dynamic to the scene and ultimately to the solution.

We also have a policy that no team member is above doing anything, as long as it's for the good of the company. You never hear the words, "That's not my job," in the halls of the BNW. If those words were spoken, they would be drowned out by the other 99 percent saying, "How can I help?"

Customer Service

We treat our customers as our "scene partners." Our job is to understand their point of view, actively and intently listen, say "yes, first," and then take action. The ultimate goal of our customer service staff is to make everyone else in the scene (the customer) look better than themselves. Both of these customer service philosophies find their origin in improvisational scene creation.

We also are very protective of our customer service employees. If a customer is treating them disrespectfully, we always support the employee's decision to leave the scene. This rarely happens, as our employees are good improvisers and have the skills to continue the scene—even with a scene partner who has a challenging point of view or attitude.

Evaluation

The key to our evaluation process is our ability to use the same vocabulary with staff that we have developed to evaluate our actors and stage productions. We are very careful to use language that separates the employee from the work during job evaluations with staff members. We make observations, not critiques. Setting clear expectations at the top of the scene (project) helps employees control and monitor their role and contributions freely. We spend much more time enabling our employees to become closer to their most productive self, rather than critiquing the path they choose to take. Like most work environments, we demand employee accountability. However, we evaluate performance in relation to the declarations of the standards and productivity identified by the employee, not management.

Honesty

At the core of all we do is honesty—honesty with our scene partners (team members and customers) and with ourselves. The only sure way to get fired from the BNW is to be dishonest. It is one expectation that cannot be compromised because our environment of trust would decay and cease to be successful. We believe that open, honest, and direct communication is the driving force behind creating and maintaining successful improvisational scenes and workplaces.

Trust

All members of the company must trust each other. We have been very successful at creating an environment that is trusting and respectful. If there is one aspect of the business that we micromanage, it is policing any drama, cliques, hidden agendas, or unresolved issues within a team. By doing this, we are able to maintain a workplace devoid of typical office politics, finger pointing, or disrespectful behavior, which, in turn, further develops a sense of trust.

Lack of Drama

All of our employees possess high levels of trust and honesty enabling us to work more efficiently as a team. There is no drama to detract us from our everyday tasks. As a result of this, employees in our workplace are able to focus 110 percent of their energies on the tasks at hand and attention is not diverted toward petty or unimportant matters. We are constantly being told that the amount of work being produced by our little theatre is disproportionate to the size of our team. We are cranking it out.

Training / Employee Orientation

We have no formal training or orientation processes for new staff members. We simply begin to immerse every new employee in the principles of improvisation and the qualities of a successful improv scene from the moment they join our team. Some new recruits are initially taken aback by the lack of structure, but they quickly come to appreciate the level of trust and confidence being given to them. They are soon inspired by the realization that everyone on the team believes in their ability to do a great job, and empowered by the level of creative safety in their new environment. The lack of an official training regimen, in effect, promotes quicker integration and increased innovation.

Acceptance of Imperfection

Improvisation is truly an imperfect art form and acceptance of this imperfection is prominent in the culture of the BNW. Although we strive to create the best scene possible and the most profitable solutions, everyone recognizes an improvisation-based entrepreneurial company will make its share of mistakes. If something shows itself to be unworkable, we recognize that we've just received a wonderful piece of information that can help us move the scene forward in a different and more positive way. It is our reaction to these "mistakes" that helps to make our workplace unique.

It is our belief that nothing *really* goes wrong; instead it goes as it should. Acceptance of imperfection allows each of us to view challenges without boundaries and recover quickly if something doesn't work as expected. When viewed as a necessary by-product and positive indicator of innovative risk-taking, accepting imperfection becomes an integral component to future success.

Management

The benefit of an improvisational management style is that it allows us to go beyond the limits of a typical job description. At any moment, team roles are changing as the entire scene (project) moves forward, and we support this change as a natural and positive progression. We address every situation as though stepping into an improv scene. We observe what's working, what's not, and determine what should be management's role, if any, in moving the scene along.

Another improvisational management technique we use is to be in constant observation of our scene partners' behavior. Specifically, we constantly, yet gently, watch for any symptoms that an employee may show as a result of burnout or some other occupational malady. We assume that all of our employees are fully committed to doing their best to improve our company. Based on that assumption, we can confidently discuss the symptoms we have observed with the employee. This practice is beneficial in maintaining our employees' level of commitment and longevity. It has also allowed us to identify when it truly is time for an employee to move on and away from the Brave New Workshop. That discovery is liberating for the employee and a tremendous cost-savings for the company.

The quality talent that drives the BNW speaks volumes about our ability to run a company using this management style. We do not expect this management style is *the* answer for you or for your company. We hope it can become a *version* of *your answer* and that you can incorporate our secrets into your workplace. Keeping true to our history, our secrets, and our philosophy, we can't tell you how to do it, but we can show you how it works for us.

Thanks for Listening

On behalf of everyone who has worked at the Brave New Workshop, thank you for reading this book. We feel honored you are interested in what we do and hope you enjoyed it.

We hoped that by writing this book we would:

- Demystify the role of improvisation in creativity and innovation.

- Give non-actors and non-improvisers a usable process to increase the quality and quantity of the ideas they produce.

- Provide a learning tool that is accessible to all types of people for all sorts of reasons.

- Play a small role in increasing the innovation of the universe by sharing secrets that we believe possess immediate and enduring benefit.

- Help the reader start a journey to their unique, most innovative self.

- Make the top one hundred books banned by the Roman Catholic Church, perhaps right below *Harry Potter*.

One final note:

Remember, again, that part of improvisation is accepting the imperfection of the art form. This is a reality for us everyday. Like lots of companies our size and in our industry, we are consistently reminded of our own imperfection. We are sometimes late on our rent, we have employees who leave on bad terms, we miss deadlines, the economy screws us too, we get angry at each other, and we make dozens of "bad" decisions each day. Still, we have been able to somehow continually produce a product our customers love. We have gained a reputation for being innovative and irreverent and constant. We have accomplished this year after year after year because we cling to the secrets we've just shared with you.

We also tend to be less hard on ourselves than most. Our creative process has shown us—way too often—that most "mistakes" lead to the next unexpected innovation, the next great idea, and the next excellent scene. We never find value in dwelling on what we did not accomplish. It seems we are most interested in what we can, and will, accomplish.

Keep laughing and, if you're in the Twin Cities, come to our theatre and laugh at us!

We leave you with this:

BRAVE NEW WORKSHOP THEATRE

DATE: 02.09.02

SHOW: Bushwhacked II: One Nation Under Stress

TITLE: "It's Hard to Be An American"

DRAFT: FINAL

PREMISE:
Folksingers sing in a charged and honest way about the trials of being from the biggest and the best country.

SETTING:
BNW stage.

CHARACTERS:
FOLKSINGERS: white, privileged, and full of conviction. Like Peter, Paul, and Mary.

PATRIOTIC SINGERS: white, privileged, and full of soul.

(Lights up on FOLKSINGERS)

FOLKSINGER I

Thanks a lot, thank you. After September 11,
I think we all started thinking about what it means
to be American. And this whole terrorist/American thing
hit all of us really hard, but I think it hit me the hardest.
You know, I ask myself everyday—why me?

FOLKSINGER 2

Why not someone else?

FOLKSINGER I

I think about me a lot—and what it means to be an American
and how goddamn hard it is to be an American . . .

FOLKSINGER 2

It's goddamn hard.

FOLKSINGERS

(Sings.)

From a mean ol' king did we escape
in search of a better way,

But those Injuns didn't just roll on over,
they said we couldn't stay

They made us fight, they made us kill,
so we did so without regret

And still we walked them to new land
and gave them free blankets

If you think it's hard to starve and
grovel, begging on the ground

Try eating scones and lattes
while losing those last five pounds

Afghanistan and Kosovo,
brown countries we invade

We are forced to bomb their evil ways
then pay for human aid

It's hard to be an American
Where freedom is already won
Nobody hugs the Superpower
Instead they scream and run
It's hard to be the privileged,
the best, the chosen few
It's not our fault that we're American
And God loves us more than you

If you thought being a slave was tough
try owning four or five

We paid for the shipping from Africa
and some didn't even survive

This is the land of opportunity
a land of plenty and great might

But it hurts to live with the stifling guilt
of knowing it's better when you're white

It's hard to be an American
Where freedom is already won
Nobody hugs the Superpower
Instead they scream and run
It's hard to be the privileged,
the best, the chosen few
It's not our fault that we're American
And God loves us more than you

(PATRIOTIC SINGERS enter with candles.)

FOLKSINGER I

You know, other countries just don't realize
how hard it is to be an American.

PATRIOT I

It's hard to know that people are so jealous of us.

PATRIOT 2

It's hard to know what to spend
my money on.

PATRIOT 3

It's hard to read about how hard the war is for other people.

FOLKSINGER I

It's hard to read.

FOLKSINGERS

(Singing.)

It's hard to be an American
Where freedom is already won

ALL

Nobody hugs the Superpower
Instead they scream and run.
It's hard to be the privileged,
the best, the chosen few
It's not our fault that we're American

FOLKSINGER I

And God loves us more than you

FOLKSINGERS

It's not our fault that we're Americans
And God loves us more than you!

(They blow out candles. Blackout or transition.)

Appendix

The Definition of Improvisation,
or This Is What We Think It Is

There are hundreds of definitions for improvisation, and several books have been written about the topic. For our purposes, I will focus on the Brave New Workshop's definition—the one that has driven our company for all these years and will continue to do so. First, it's important to know that our definition is borne from the firm belief that absolutely anyone can improvise if they allow themselves to play. For every person who has ever entered the doors of our theatre, trained in our improv classes, participated in one of our corporate services events, or even laughed as part of our theatre audience, we believe the art of improvisation has the ability to help them find their most creative and innovative self.

At the BNW, we define improvisation as "an attitude that allows one person, or a group of people, to innovate and create instantly by using their own sense of trust, truth, acceptance, and creativity." Pure improvisation can happen only when the group works as a team, and ideas and actions flow freely without judgment. Improvisation IS NOT about being the quickest, smartest, being the funniest, or being right.

When the BNW views improvisation as a tool of professional development for employees, managers, and companies in a business environment, we take our definition a step beyond theatrical performance. We've learned, and recognized, that improvisation and the professional environment have a lot in common: both rely on individuals to work as a team towards an end product or solution; both require individuals to listen, trust, give and take, share ideas, and create; and both face problems when individuals do not exhibit or practice effective leadership and team play. Improvisation is a powerful model for the professional environment. When improvisation works it is because the individual members improvising together have agreed upon a set of behaviors and philosophies, and they consistently adhere to them. When this "spontaneous agreement" occurs in a workplace setting, it is creatively magical, amazingly powerful, and undeniably effective in building better teams.

The History of Improvisation

The are many versions of the history of improvisational theatre. Each version cites slightly different origins. Despite this, there are a few people who are synonymous with its creation, including Viola Spolin, Dudley Riggs, Paul Sills, Del Close, David Shepherd, and Keith Johnstone. That said, there were probably several others who also explored unique ways of interacting with audiences, not unlike theatrical improvisation. To them, I apologize for not knowing who they are. The following timeline highlights some of the most widely recognized contributors to modern day improvisation and should give you a taste for how the art form developed.

Europe, mid-1500s	Nearly all histories of improvisation mention Commedia Del'Arte as the oldest ancestor to modern day improvisation. In Europe, Commedia Del'Arte featured traveling entertainers who performed, within a scene, entirely improvised dialogue.
Chicago, 1933	Viola Spolin develops a new style of instruction based on the belief that children would be more likely to enjoy acting classes if the main points were learned through games. Her son, Paul Sills, continues his mother's work at the University of Chicago in the mid-1950s. He later works with Del Close and David Shepherd (see 1955 below).

1946   The Young Actor's Company, using the principles of Spolin, is founded.

1952   Dudley Riggs founds the Instant Theatre Company in New York City, based on the comedy of vaudeville. As part of its growth, the troupe begins asking audiences for suggestions during performances. In 1959, the Instant Theatre Company makes its way to Minneapolis and is renamed the Brave New Workshop in 1961. The theatre soon becomes home to improvisation in the Twin Cities and remains one of the few satirical comedy theatres in the country.

1955   Del Close and David Shepherd work with Sills to create an ensemble-acting troupe that would appeal to the average Joe. The group they form is called The Compass Players. In 1959, this group is the foundation for establishing Second City in Chicago, still famously running today.

1960   The Premise opens in New York, Washington, and London; closes in 1963.

1963   The Committee is formed in Los Angeles and San Francisco and gives birth to a variety of companies that succeed it.

1964   El Teatro Campasino, plays in Delano, California, for a bit.

Late 60s,   Keith Johnstone, then teaching at the University of Calearly 70s   gary, combines the work of Viola Spolin with the audience elements and passion of sports to develop a unique form of improvisation. His work creates Theatre-sports, and over the next several years leagues develop in New York, Seattle, Washington, and Orlando as well as in many other cities and quite a few foreign countries. Its most recent incarnation is The Actor's New School in New York City, founded in 1990.

1968	The Fourth Wall plays for a couple of years in New York City.
1969	The Proposition begins in Boston and continues today.
1975	Off the Wall plays in Los Angeles until 1999.
1976	The Groundlings begin productions, also in LA, and remain active.
1976	War Babies LA, opens and then closes in 1986.
1983	Improv Olympic is formed and still operating.
1984	The Wims start (and stop) playing in LA.
Present Day	There are thousands of improvisation groups across the globe!

As you can see, one of the common characteristics of the improv industry is its short life span. It is one of the reasons I feel so strongly about sharing the Brave New Workshop's creative process. Dudley's humble humor, keen satirical insight, boundless creativity, and circus-bred spontaneity kept the theatre running for more than forty years and are the foundation of his legacy on which we will continue to build.

If you are interested in learning more about how the Brave New Workshop can help you, your organization or company to be more innovative please go to:

www.BraveNewWorkshop.com

or

www.SpeedofLaughter.com